Thomas Weil

New Grammar
of Ornament

Lars Müller Publishers

Table of Contents

The *New Grammar of Ornament* and the Geometric Ornament as Art's Original Language

Thomas Weil

FOUR PROTO-ORNAMENTS: The earliest ornamented artifacts were found in southern Africa. These were linear engravings on stones, ostrich eggshells and ochre blocks, as well as "decorations" with dots. The linear engravings were arranged in stripes or rectangular or triangular shapes, whereas the dots generally had a free arrangement. These four proto-ornaments – striped, rectangular and triangular lines and freely arranged dots – have continued as the typological and constructive basis throughout the history of ornament from that time to the present day. The ornamental principles have proven to be an internalized strategy and anthropological constant. My *New Grammar of Ornament* builds upon this knowledge starting from these four original ornament types. Ornaments are based on the arrangement or correlation of shapes that are identical or similar. A physiological reason for their use might lie in the fact, as determined by brain research, that our brain rewards the construction of ordered arrangements by releasing hormones. Ornaments reflect not least archetypical images, the interpretation of which point to ritual religious areas and dream research.

HISTORY: The four proto-ornaments were first discovered in southern Africa around 70,000 BCE and in Europe around 40,000 BCE. These marked the beginning of a global culture of ornamentation that unfolded both in tribal societies and in advanced civilizations such as Egypt, Greece, Rome and China. Geometric ornamentation assumes special significance within the Islamic cultural sphere as a result of the absence of figural images. There is a vast abundance of ornaments worldwide that have been created on all continents and in all the different cultures, epochs and social strata, with the most varied materials. When modernity as influenced by the West gradually began to unfold,[1] ornament enjoyed a heyday in excess. Furthered by the options available through industrial production and publication, the ornament spread out tentacles into all areas of design in the nineteenth century. The Austrian architect Adolf Loos responded to this development in his renowned text by equating "ornament and crime."[2] In the modern age of the twentieth century, this became a creed of sorts: The ornament was now considered the enemy of all good design. It nevertheless lived on as a geometric architectural principle of construction and, in a different way, in art, in order finally to be rehabilitated in postmodernity. Today the use of computers again fosters an inflationary treatment of the ornament, as anyone can transform anything imaginable into stereotypical ornaments with the click of a mouse.

ON THE STRUCTURE OF THE BOOK

TITLE: The title is a reference to the seminal work *The Grammar of Ornament* by Owen Jones, written in 1856. (See p. 13.)

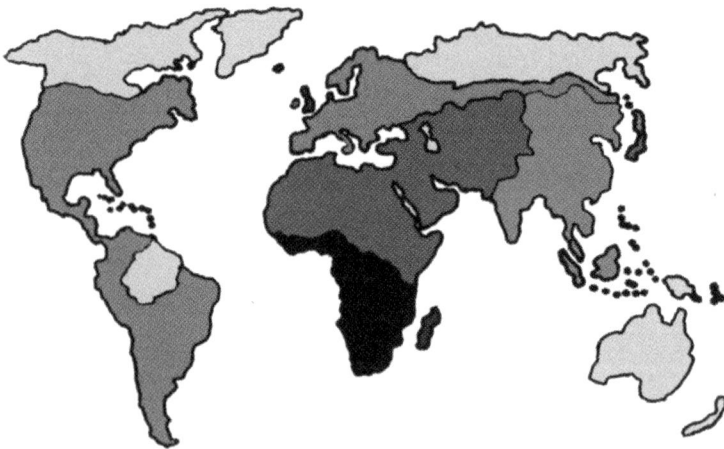

Global Ornament Spheres:
The five spheres of ornament: European, Islamic, Sub-Saharan, Far Eastern, Indigenous

4

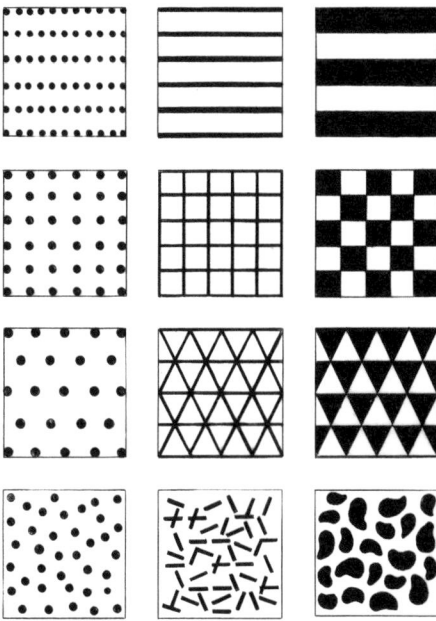

Dot, Line, Plane:
Striped, Rectangular, Triangular, Free Order

MINIMAL, GEOMETRIC, FLORAL:
The book is divided into three main sections with the categories of ornaments: MINIMAL, GEOMETRIC and FLORAL. The first two categories are applied to the four simple proto-ornaments with their STRIPED, RECTANGULAR, TRIANGULAR and FREE ORDERS. These four types of arrangement in turn are each subdivided according to the three established forms of presentation as WITH DOTS, WITH LINES and WITH PLANES. The main sections MINIMAL and GEOMETRIC thus each consist of twelve parts, whereby GEOMETRIC, with its more complex geometry, draws in particular from Hellenistic, Persian/Islamic, Medieval/European and Chinese models. The third part, FLORAL, refers to floral ornaments, the first of which go back more than 6000 years. From the forms used again and again worldwide, four basic types have been identified: Blossoms viewed from the front (SUNS), purely plant motifs (PLANTS), abstract motifs (ARCHETYPES) and the earth with its ornamental manifestations such as water waves, clouds, fire and landscape (EARTH). Since the linear arrangement is the most customary one, the subdivision into dots, lines and planes will be omitted here.

CHAPTER CONTENTS: The three main sections, MINIMAL, GEOMETRIC and FLORAL, will be introduced by striking full-page images, the POETICS and an introductory text. Each of the three main sections is subdivided into twelve chapters. Each chapter begins with a black-and-white pilot graphic explaining the contents, as well as a text and an appropriate photograph from everyday life or a design drawing. This is followed by the illustrations. In the main section, MINIMAL, the most minimal versions of illustrations are mentioned in the image captions.

ILLUSTRATIONS: Except for a few examples from Europe, the Middle and Far East and Africa (identified in the figure captions), all ornament illustrations were created by the author: as sketches in MINIMAL, constructed in GEOMETRIC and as an outline graphic in FLORAL. The six primary colors (red, yellow, blue, green, orange, violet), supplemented with black, white, gray and brown, assure a balanced color scheme. All illustrations generally have only two colors, in order not to be unnecessarily distracting. Criteria for the selection of the examples were: the options for an open order, for varied readings, and the author's practice-trained conscience as an artist. The open nature enables the user to think of variants for every illustration.

GUEST CONTRIBUTORS: The archaeologist and paleoanthropologist Manuel Will takes up the notion of the ornament as an anthropological constant. He considers the earliest art forms and offers a concise survey of ornaments that were created as early as the Stone Age in Africa and Europe. On the basis of terminological differentiation revolving around the term "ornament," the art theorist and critic Heinz Schütz presents an excursus into the history of ornament from a Western perspective in order to focus on the range of meanings associated with the ornament.

1   In the fine arts, the modern age experienced an initial highpoint as early as 1870 with Impressionism; the beginning of the literary modern age came with Naturalism (1880), and modern approaches in architecture were already noted in Classicism. The linking of the program of Art Deco and the Arts and Crafts Movement, art and life, laid the foundation for the avant-gardism of the early twentieth century.

2   Adolf Loos, Ornament and Crime: Selected Essays, trans. Michael Mitchell (Riverside, CA: Ariadne, 1998); or Adolf Loos, Ornament and Crime: Thoughts on Design and Materials, trans. Shaun Whiteside (London: Penguin 2019).

The Archaeology and Origins of Ornaments: A Deep-Time Perspective

Manuel Will, University of Tübingen

Archaeology is the study of human history and society by examining past people's material culture that survived in the ground for centuries and millennia. This work takes on particular prominence for periods without written language, which applies to all societies older than 5000 years. Today we know from genetic, anthropological and archaeological research that our species, *Homo sapiens*, originated about 200,000–300,000 years ago (= 200–300 ka) on the African continent. The study of these earliest periods of our existence, the archaeology of the Stone Age or Paleolithic period, provides a unique, deep-time perspective to trace our past without access to written sources by excavating and studying artifacts that have been preserved until today. By uncovering the earliest historical archive of our species, spanning the longest period of time, Paleolithic archaeology constitutes the beginnings of our culture, language and art. It also provides a means to track the first use of ornaments – the topic of this book – including their age, forms, development and function.

however, these are preceded by much earlier evidence from the Stone Age. The oldest abstract engravings on various materials such as rocks and pigments date back at least 100 ka in Africa. Magnificent cave paintings and carefully shaped figurines of animals and humans dating back 40 ka have been found frequently around the globe. In the following, a short overview of early ornaments in the Stone Age of Africa and Europe will be presented, with a focus on the ornament theory that is developed in this book. Manifold connections can be found between modern-day and prehistoric ornaments in their basic form and shape. Even more, the elementary geometric forms hypothesized as the basis for all ornaments here all appear in the Paleolithic archaeological record. Archaeology thus provides some independent empirical backing for the grammar of ornaments proposed here, and a potential explanation for this continuity in our species over tens of thousands of years until today will be discussed at the end of the present book.

Homo sapiens originated in Africa. The archaeological time period of these earliest modern humans is called the Middle Stone Age (MSA). The MSA harbors the oldest ornament examples, which date between 50 and 70 ka ago and include different media. For one, early humans scored pieces of ochre – a natural earth pigment with high amounts of iron oxide – with various shapes and patterns of lines. The most famous piece comes from Blombos Cave, a site located on the southern coastline of South Africa. Here, about 70 ka ago, early humans scored a rectangular block of red ochre with various patterns, including

Fig. 1   Engraved ochre with isosceles triangles and parallel lines from Blombos

How old is the oldest archaeological evidence for art, symbols and ornaments? Many people would associate the earliest works of great art with the first civilizations, such as ancient Greece or Egypt. In reality,

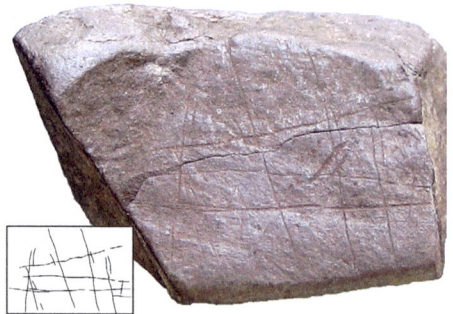

Fig. 2   Engraved ochre with grid from Klein Kliphuis

isosceles triangles that form an X pattern enclosed by parallel lines (figure 1). Further examples of engraved red ochre from this region exist. They include a grid consisting of multiple lines on a small piece excavated at the site of Klein Kliphuis on the Western Cape of South Africa, dated a bit later to circa 50–60 ka ago (figure 2).

Various engravings of similar age that are even more remarkable have been found in two cave sites in South Africa in the last decade. What makes these patterns so outstanding is both their medium and the variety of forms: Early humans engraved the shells of ostrich eggs with multiple arrangements of lines and dots. At the cave site of Diepkloof, where these artifacts were first found, recognizable motifs include parallel and sub-parallel lines as well as hatched bands and crosshatched grids, sometimes associated with more or less parallel lines of dots (figure 3). Hundreds of only centimeter-size fragments have been discovered at Diepkloof. These patterns had originally made up the exterior decoration of flasks used for carrying water or other drinkable liquids. What is even more striking, archaeologists subsequently found these ornaments at another site, Klipdrift Rockshelter, several hundred kilometers from Diepkloof along the southern coast

of South Africa. Astonishingly, the same varieties of decorations were found again on ostrich eggshell fragments, here also including isosceles triangles forming X marks (figure 3). This is evidence of a tradition of ornament-making in our species as early as tens of thousands of years ago.

About 60 ka ago, humans dispersed from Africa to the rest of the world. Our forebears reached Europe about 45 ka ago and eventually replaced the Neanderthals already living there. The initial colonization of Ice Age Europe saw an explosion of art and symbols in the archaeological record. These artistic expressions can be found on cave walls and portable pebbles. They further include small figurines carved of mammoth ivory and animal bones depicting various animals and, rarely, humans. This period of human history is called the Upper Paleolithic. In the following, only a small selection from the vast record of this time is discussed and illustrated, exemplifying the overall range of Ice Age art and decorations. The earliest settlements of modern humans in Europe, the so-called Aurignacian period, features finely made artwork in Germany, France, Italy and Spain. The Swabian Jura in southwest Germany was one of the centers of Ice Age art, featuring its earliest expressions between circa 35 and 43 ka ago that led to its inscription as a UNESCO World Heritage Site in 2017. Here, early members of our species carved abstract signs and various markings on the earliest animal and human figurines. These ornaments contain parallel lines, isosceles triangles forming X marks, parallel dot rows and mixtures of these motifs (figure 4). In most cases, the decorations cannot be explained as simple illustrations of fur or hunting wounds of the carved animals, but were intentionally applied for some other reason. As just one example, some of the mammoth figurines bear X marks on the soles of their feet. A famous human depiction on a piece of ivory from the site of Geissenklösterle in the Swabian Jura features four rows of parallel dots on the reverse whose meaning remains debated. Many of the famous cave paintings of the Ice Age in Spain and France at sites such as Altamira, Chauvet and Lascaux also bear a variety of the abovementioned ornament patterns in the Aurignacian and subsequent time periods alongside their famous animal depictions.

Excavations in the Swabian Jura once

Fig. 3   Composition of engraved ostrich eggshell fragments with various decorations from Diepkloof

Fig. 4   Various abstract designs on animal figurines from the Swabian Jura

cups in various geometric arrangements, as well as abundant grids and latticework composed of multiple lines with right-angled intersections (figures 6 and 7). This list could be endlessly continued into the later periods of human history.

In sum, this brief overview of the earliest art and ornaments made by our species in the Paleolithic era provides a unique source of data to trace and understand the creative and artistic skills of our earliest ancestors. As should be evident from the description and illustration of these motifs, the Paleolithic ornaments conform closely to all of the shapes proposed in this book as the fundamental building blocks of geometric ornaments up to modern times. The difference is mostly one of frequency and medium used, but the resemblance is intriguing and spans tens of thousands of years. As such, this practice of creating specific geometric ornaments can be called an anthropological constant. Yet how can we explain this astonishing continuity? It is difficult to imagine the knowledge on creating these patterns being shared across thousands of years and kilometers in the Stone Age among scattered hunter-gatherer groups. The motifs also transcend a number of ecologies (steppes, forests, semideserts,

again uncovered mobile art, this time from sometime later in the Magdalenian period, dated to circa 12–17 ka ago, in the form of river pebbles and limestone bearing traces of decorations. Most interesting in this context are stones with two parallel rows of dots applied with

Fig. 5   Red dot rows on limestone and pebbles from the Swabian Jura

paint from red ochre that can be found at several sites (figure 5). From a bit later in time, in the so-called Mesolithic period at circa 5–10 ka ago, numerous sites in France in the Fontainebleau region have produced cave walls full of decorations. This rock art includes cupules, carved-out

tundra, etc.), media (rock, ochre, ostrich eggshell, bone, ivory, etc.) and art forms (cave walls, figurines, portable stones). This fact precludes any one-to-one correspondence with a particular function or meaning. A potential explanation for the perplexing consistency can be found in the ways

Fig. 6 & 7   Latticework, lines and dot patterns from Fontainebleau

related to *Homo sapiens* in its entirety, a comparative and global perspective is required that spans the entire history of our species, which only archaeology can provide. As such, this book and its new grammar of ornaments can serve as a meaningful and elegant bridge between our deepest past in the Paleolithic period and our current postmodern times. Future archaeological research might someday even help to further elaborate current theories.

our human brains work(ed) and the so-called "entoptic phenomena." According to archaeologist David Lewis-Williams, entoptic forms are visual phenomena experienced by humans that derive from the brain's specific neurology and result from states of altered consciousness such as intoxication, trance or light deprivation. These entoptic phenomena include parallel and zigzagging lines as well as latticework and dot patterns, fitting with many – though not all – of the abovementioned archaeo-logical patterns and the basic building blocks of the ornament theory developed here. As these forms appear to be hard-wired in our brains and not dependent on any particular external visual experiences, they can crosscut various cultures and societies and might thus explain the consis-tency of decorations used.

This short overview demonstrates the importance of archaeology as the empi-rical underpinning of the ornament theory developed here and could have easily continued up to the first literate societies. When examining cultural phenomena

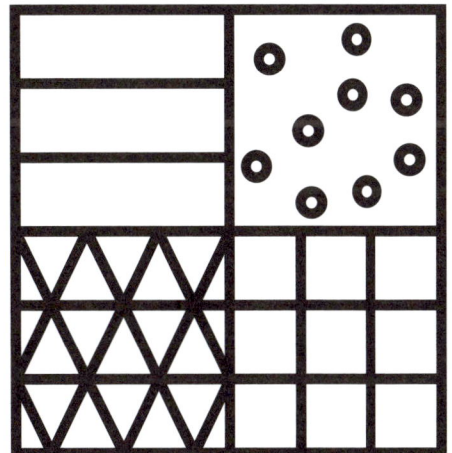

Decorum. Ornament. Pattern. Art

Heinz Schütz

They have no practical purpose and do not serve as containers for the ashes of the deceased. The stone urns are frequently decorated with stone draperies. Just as the stone draperies simulate fabric, the stone vessel here functions as a sculpture and a simulation of an urn. This simulation is the result of a process of defunctionalization and ornamentalization. The process begins when the form of a vessel receives greater attention than its practical use, and it continues when the vessels are produced and displayed as ostentatious showpieces due to their décor, their

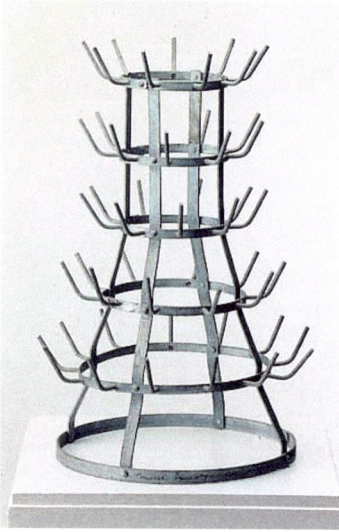

Marcel Duchamp's *Bottle Rack* (Porte-Bouteille) in the National Gallery of Modern and Contemporary Art, Rome

Funeral urn at St. Georg's cemetery, Munich

0. BOTTLE RACK AND URN

Bottle racks are everyday objects. At the beginning of the last century, the French-American avant-garde artist Marcel Duchamp declared a bottle rack to be a readymade. In other words, he took a functional object that he did not create, but was instead manufactured, and declared it to be a work of art. Viewing a bottle rack as art changes the way it is perceived. The default expectation is that art depicts something specific, prompting the question: What does the bottle rack represent? The answer is: Itself. Viewing it draws attention to its form: circular bands stacked over each other with barb-like rows of hooks. The form is a result of its function and does not prove useful until empty bottles are placed onto the hooks, something ruled out in the context of museums, in which Duchamp's readymade became an icon of avant-garde art. As art, the bottle rack has been defunctionalized, presenting itself as an absurd, mysterious, fetish-like construct.

Antiqued stone urns and stone amphorae often crown the tombstone architecture at old cemeteries.

ornamentation and images. The process proceeds a step further when the vessel decorates the architecture and the architecture places the vessel at center stage. In that case the vessel serves not only as an ornament carrier, but it becomes an ornament itself. Once defunctionalized, an urn at the cemetery becomes a grave ornament.

1. DECORUM AND ORNAMENT

If we compare the use of the "bottle rack" with that of the "urn," it is apparent that the "bottle rack," at least initially, is indeed deliberately disturbing and confusing within an art context, whereas the "urn" affirms the tradition it draws upon in order to mark the site as dignified and appropriate. From a historical perspective, the question of appropriateness is key and an inherent aspect of the ornament.

The Eurocentric debate on ornaments is often traced back to Leon Battista Alberti, who as a Renaissance humanist in turn refers to Vitruvius's books on architecture.[1] Both consider the term "decorum," borrowed from the area of rhetoric.

Alberti defines the term "decorum" in the sense of "appropriate." In his view, it is a decisive measure for successful architecture. Through decorum a building is connected to social demands and norms. In the sense of decorum, architecture contributes to the construction of the public sphere and it participates in enacting social hierarchies, public institutions, and social differences. This also includes distinguishing between different types of buildings with respect to their significance in society as a whole. Within this context, the ornament assumes an important role and decorates, in the sense of the default of decorum, community-related architectural structures such as temples, basilica, theaters and arches of triumph. Regarding private buildings, on the other hand, Alberti calls for restraint. For him, the important thing is always the harmonic accord between the building and its parts, the ornaments and the building's function.

When considering the terms *decorum*, *decor* and *ornamentum*, semantic overlapping and differences become apparent. Decorum, in the sense of "that which is befitting," means "appropriateness," "decency," "propriety." *Decor*, like *ornamentum*, can mean "grace," "decoration," and "adornment," but *ornamentum* additionally means "preciousness," "accoutrement," "outfitting." If we take into account that *ornamentum* is also used in the sense of "a mark of distinction," "insignias," and "esteem," a social dimension of appreciation linking *decorum* and *ornamentum* is revealed.

Alberti gives the ornament a role of its own, but he views it nevertheless as an "attached or additional"[2] art form and a "mere ingredient." If we detach ourselves from the historical discourse on the architectural ornament, we open up an inexhaustible field of objects connected to the ornament. It is interwoven in clothing and engraved into the body as a tattoo. It is linked to cult objects and everyday commodities, to vessels, carpets and furniture, to tools, instruments and weapons. It frames pictures, is rampant in books and on floors, walls and ceilings. It decorates boats, carriages, saddles, poles and lanterns. Accordingly, ornaments are created with and in a vast range of materials. They are drawn, printed, painted, chiseled, lathed, embossed, punched, carved, engraved, braided, woven, pottered, knitted, forged, cast, laced, scored, needled, knotted, and vectored.

Whereas everyday objects serve a purpose, the ornament, as a decorative addition, has no direct practical use, especially from the perspective of a functionalist modernity that rejected ornamentation. And yes, depending on the dominant worldview, the use of ornaments and signs can be attributed a functionality within the scope of a purpose-oriented practice. In the sense of magical-religious thought, as was practiced especially by early societies, ornaments and signs are used to conjure transcendental forces. They serve, for example, as defensive magic, as symbols to encourage fertility, as a ritual war paint or as a tribal sign to indicate ethnic affiliation and social difference. This manifestation has been assumed by flags and crests in younger societies, while crests in turn have mutated to brand logos in capitalist consumer society. Script ornaments of today's graffiti tags function as personalized logos as it were, through which the writers publicize their names and mark the public space.

Ornaments have a potential intrinsic force that appears extrinsically as a force of transfiguration on that which is decorated. Let us consider, for example, a simple, nonornamented sacral onyx chalice. If it is set and embellished with gold ornaments and precious gems, we can consider this a response to its sacral value, which is enacted through the transfiguring force of the ornament. In this way ornaments can resemble performative speech acts. Just as performative speech acts create something by uttering it, the ornament as an adornment serves to increase the significance of that which is adorned. A frequently cited performative example is "I hereby baptize you." This act of generating meaning has sociopolitical effects. For example, a king is entitled to his vestments, but it is the vestments that allow a king to appear as a king. The power of ornamental transfiguration that comes from the adornments and from the gold and marble of the royal palaces continue to have an effect today, such as when dictators and semidictators imitate the palatial style in order to heighten their self-enacted importance. Their anachronistic recourse–

Onyx chalice of Doña Urraca from the church treasure of the Basilica of San Isidoro in León

especially against the foil of democratic social orders–is the opposite of that which was once called "decorum" in the ornament debate.

2. ORNAMENT AND PATTERN

Patterns can be ornaments, but not every pattern is an ornament and not all ornaments are patterns. Repetition and repeatability are the key principles on which patterns are based. In this sense the term is used broadly, in areas ranging as far as thought and behavior patterns. In the context of ornaments, "pattern" can refer to a draft or template that is reproduced again and again. However, "pattern" also refers to the design, the repetitive arrangement of motifs and shapes – an arrangement that in turn generates an overarching structure, usually a rhythmic metastructure composing the whole.

Ornaments become widespread by means of patterns as models that circulate in templates and sample books. They were first reproduced and created by artisans and artists, and later, since the nineteenth century, increasingly by industrial machines. The ornament templates function like rhetorical formulas that overlay objects and architectures, letting them speak a common language. However, this language has been increasingly diverging from the old forms dating back to antiquity, becoming multilingual in the nineteenth century. This development is determined by the historicizing recourse to a wide range of styles, by interest in ornaments of other ethnic groups, and by demands for contemporary innovation and the associated clearing out of antiquated ornamental forms. These forms were nevertheless still used beyond the nineteenth century. Even in the twenty-first century, cheap styrofoam versions of decorative moldings, for example, are still sold in home-improvement centers for DIYers.

Patterns emerge through the additive multiplication of a motif; they tend toward endless repetition that is limited only by the borders of the patterned surface. The desire for repetition is also pronounced in relation to ornaments in general, even individual stand-alone motifs arranged symmetrically such that two identical halves mirror each other. There are also ornaments that can appear not only as a pattern but separately as well, such as the asymmetrical rocaille, which like an invader takes over every conceivable position in a space, even forming objects such as lecterns, pulpits and confessionals to match its style. And not least, patterns have a specific tendency to be flat or at least to be perceived in reference to a surface.

Ornaments and patterns share their own logic, which the motifs and modes of representation must follow. Self-referential geometric shapes are used, as well as figurative flora and fauna motifs, which as images refer to something with which they have a perceptible resemblance. Furthermore, the shapes and motifs used can be symbolically charged. In the fog of history the original meaning thus gets lost through long-term use as an ornament or, if still known, it becomes irrelevant or reinterpreted in the new cultural context. The ornamentalization of symbolic signs, their being strung together in continued repetition, allows its meaning to fade until it vanishes entirely in favor of its function as a pattern. Even regarding image motifs used as ornaments, due to the stylization the presentation becomes more important than that which is depicted.[3]

The nineteenth century was the heyday of ornamentation, when the term was redefined such that "pattern" and "ornament" became synonymous. This time also marked "the transition from 'ornament' and 'handicraft' to 'patterns' and 'design.'"[4] The pattern shifted toward design and two-dimensionality. One of the most influential books on ornaments, *The Grammar of Ornament* by Owen Jones, was first published in 1856 and continues to be reprinted to this day.[5] It was the first to offer an extensive collection of ornaments from various epochs and cultural spheres. In his plates, Jones abstracts the materials with which, and the objects on which, the ornaments are created. Transformed onto a flat surface, they become patterns for "bodiless ornaments" – to borrow a term from Isabelle Frank.[6] With an eye toward Jones's broad conceptual understanding of ornaments, Martin Kirves assessed that "the ornamental design is in fact the ornament that serves as the model for its mechanical reproduction."[7]

Owen Jones pursued the upgrading and reinterpretation of the ornament. He criticized the "system of copying and misapplying the received forms of beauty of every bygone style of Art" and called for "an Art in harmony with our present wants and means of production."[8] Ornaments, which were consistently viewed as coordinate or subordinate, became his main focus: "A new architecture could only emerge from ornament, as Owen Jones, the architect responsible for the interior decoration of the Crystal Palace, emphasized. Ornament was, he said, the soul of the building."[9] The upgrading and

Byzantine, Chinese, Italian, Moresque
from: Owen Jones, *The Grammar of Ornament*, London 1856

reinterpretation of the ornament can be observed in various nuances, such as: (1) when Gottfried Semper no longer saw it as a "mere ingredient," but instead declared it to be the "primeval art form," which is practiced in weaving and braiding;[10] (2) when Jones's ornament collection anticipated certain concepts of a universal reception and historiography of art, albeit from a Eurocentric claim to superiority; (3) when Alois Riegl declared the style history of the ornament to be the indicator of the history of the epochs; and last but not least, (4) when the ornament is declared to be an independent artistic practice: "In that Jones attributed artistic principles to ornamentation, he elevated it to a fourth art form on a par with architecture, sculpture and painting."[11] Moreover, Alfred Lichtwark declared: "The ornament is no longer something self-evident, which everyone possesses. It no longer naively emerges as in earlier periods; it is made, it is an artistic performance like all others."[12] The upgrading of the ornament marked a step toward abstract art. Wilhelm Worringer, whose writings promoted this transition, wrote in 1907 about ornamentation: "It ought to constitute the point of departure and the fundament of all aesthetic consideration of art. ... Instead, figurative art is one-sidedly preferred as the so-called higher art."[13]

3. PATTERN AND ART

The production of ornaments is based on the distinction between draft and template on the one hand, and handcrafted or machine production on the other. In other words, design work and practical application are not carried out by the same person. This division of labor contradicts the predominant understanding of art in modernity, which views art as an expression of individual geniuses who create and sign their originals with their own hand. This lack of singularity and handwriting, and in particular the decorative function attributed to it and its connection to everyday objects, lead to ornaments being assigned a place not in the area of free arts, but that of applied arts. And yet the ornament plays a significant role in the art of the twentieth century. In contrast to the synonymous usage of "ornament" and "pattern" in the nineteenth century, the two terms need to be distinguished in the new context. Pattern now refers in particular to a construction created through repetition, a construction relieved of all decorative demands and repeatedly used in a puristic geometric form as a grid. And yet, the ornament as a precoded form of decoration also exists in the art of the twentieth century.

The nineteenth-century approaches to overcome the divide between art and applied or utility art found – beyond the all-encroaching excess of ornamentation – a puristically clarified continuation in early twentieth-century Russian constructivism, Bauhaus and De Stijl. Piet Mondrian developed a comprehensive concept for De Stijl that included both art and architecture. In an extreme reduction, he limited himself to the primary colors red, blue and yellow, and horizontal and vertical lines, with which he created irregular grid structures that organized the arrangement of the colors on walls and canvases. This abstract-universal elementarism is found in another form in the works and theoretical approach of Wassily Kandinsky at Bauhaus. He brought art back to its abstract foundations and reflected on the relationship between point, line and plane as grammatical prerequisites for painting.[14] "Elementaristic" artists such as Mondrian view the "grid," as

Rosalind E. Krauss keenly put it, as "a staircase to the Universal, and they are not interested in what happens below in the Concrete."[15]

Patterns and grids emerged in the art of the second half of the twentieth century in a different light. They appear within the scope of an artistic program that claims to be antimimetic, antisymbolic, antinarrative, antiillusionistic and antiexpressive. This program is closely connected to Clement Greenberg's flatness postulate that "the picture plane itself grows shallower and shallower,"[16] a statement which brings to mind at least superficially the flatness of Owen Jones's ornaments. Frank Stella is one of the artists of the twentieth century who celebrates flatness. His pattern pictures consist of thinly applied black bands of paint; the fine lines separating them are actually gaps in the paint on the canvas surface. The rhythm of the painted bands create the pattern that is the underlying concept. The meaning of the conception becomes even stronger in the image patterns and 3D grid structures of conceptual artist Sol Lewitt: "When an artist uses a conceptual form of art, it means that all of the planning and decisions are made beforehand and the execution is a perfunctory affair. The idea becomes a machine that makes the art."[17]

Here the "conceptual machine" takes the place of the expression and individual handwriting in modernism. In her grid pictures that are painted and drawn with extreme concentration, Agnes Martin shows how the objectivity of grids can become the contemplative challenge to artistic subjectivity. At a very different level, the "conceptual machine" in Andy Warhol's "Factory" becomes a reproduction apparatus. In response to a world determined by industrial and medial reproduction, he uses the serial reproduction of pictures of newspapers, movie stars and soup cans to ornamentalize brands and icons of consumer society. In the 1970s some American artists formed a group called Patterns and Decorations. Their goal was to reclaim the decorativeness and emotionality that minimalism had stripped from ornaments, and to bring together art that is free and applied, high and low, culturally close and distant. Their appropriations indicate what would then characterize the 1980s: the postmodern ornamentalization of modernity, which has led to a still ongoing renaissance of ornamentation in architecture, art and design, as a digital tool and as a tattoo on skin.

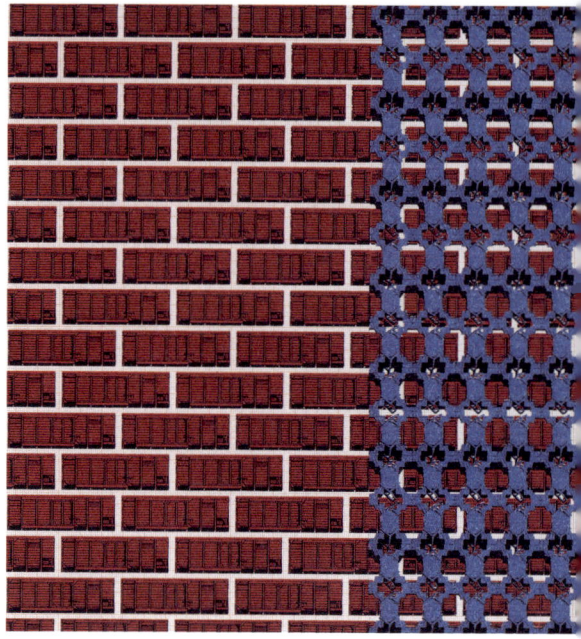

Stephan Huber, *Nordwand*, 1998

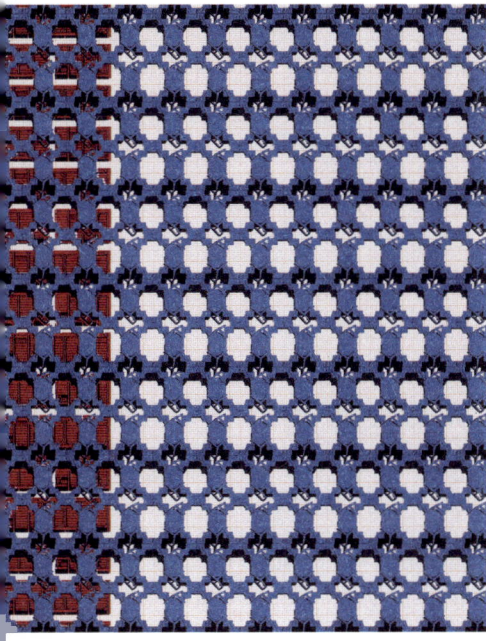

1 Leon Battista Alberti: *De re aedificatoria* (On the Art of Building), Florence 1485; Marcus Vitruvius Pollio: *De Architectura libri decem*, Rome between 33 and 22 BCE.

2 "… beauty is some inherent property, to be found suffused all through the body of that which may be called beautiful: whereas ornament, rather than being inherent, has the character of something attached or additional." Leon Battista Alberti: *On the Art of Building (in Ten Books)*, trans. Joseph Rykwert, Neil Leach, Robert Tavernor (Cambridge, MA: MIT Press, 1988), here: Book Six (2:93–94), 156.

3 "Stylization": "The direct imitation of nature, retaining form and color as much as possible, leads to the naturalistic conception; the construction of an ornament according to the rules of rhythm and symmetry, with a stricter regularity than offered by the natural motifs they are based on, is known as 'stylization.'" Naturalistic motifs are often stylized beyond recognition." Franz Sales Meyer, *Handbook of Ornament* (New York: Dover, [1957] 2018), 34–35 [English translation edited].

4 Martin Kirves: *Das Ornament als Erkenntnisform. Die epistemische Entwurfstheorie der South Kensington School*, 2019, 30; DOI: https://doi.org/10.11588/artdok.00006575.

5 Owen Jones: *The Grammar of Ornament*, London 1856.

6 Isabelle Frank: "Das körperlose Ornament im Werk von Owen Jones und Alois Riegl," in *Die Rhetorik des Ornaments*, ed. Isabelle Frank and Freia Härtung (Munich: Fink, 2001), 77–100.

7 Martin Kirves 2019, 32.

8 "Owen Jones, *The Grammar of Ornament*, chap. 12, 159, https://archive.org/details/grammarornamento0Jone

9 Martin Kirves, "Owen Jones and the Threefold Nature of Ornament," in *Ornament Today: Digital Material Structural*, ed. Jörg H. Gleiter, trans. Henry Martin and Steven Lindberg (Bozen: Bozen University Press, 2012), 44–61, here: 45; see also Martin Kirves 2019, 27.

10 Semper commented on what he saw as a close connection between weaving, braiding, ornament and architecture in his book, first published in German in 1860, Gottfried Semper, *Style in the Technical and Tectonic Arts, Or, Practical Aesthetics*, trans. Harry Francis Mallgrave and Michael Robinson (Los Angeles: Getty, 2004), here: 113, 416.

11 Isabelle Frank 2001, 87.

12 Alfred Lichtwark: "Das Ornament der Kleinmeister," *Jahrbuch Der Königlich Preussischen Kunstsammlungen* 5 (1884), 78–99, https://www.jstor.org/stable/4301778 [last accessed 13 July 2021].

13 Wilhelm Worringer, *Abstraction and Empathy*, trans. Michael Bullock (Chicago: Ivan R. Dee/Elephant Paperbacks, 1997), chapter 3 "Ornament," 51.

14 Wassily Kandinsky: *Point and Line to Plane: Contribution to the Analysis of the Pictorial Elements*, trans. Howard Dearstyne and Hilla Rebay, Bauhaus books, vol. 9, new ed. (Zurich: Lars Müller, 2021), 77.

15 Rosalind E. Krauss: "Grids," in Rosalind E. Krauss, *The Originality of The Avant-Garde and Other Modernist Myths* (Cambridge, MA, and London: MIT Press, 1985), 10; first published in October 9 (Summer 1979), 50–64.

16 Clement Greenberg: "Towards a Newer Laocoon," in *Pollock and After: the Critical Debate*, ed. Francis Frascina, 2nd ed. (New York and London: Routledge, 2000), 60–70, here: 68; first published in Partisan Review 7 (4), July/August 1940, 296–310.

17 Sol Lewitt: "Paragraphs on Conceptual Art," in *Conceptual Art: A Critical Anthology*, ed. Alexander Alberro and Blake Stimson (Cambridge, MA, and London: MIT Press, 1999), 12–16; first published in *Artforum* 5 (10), 1967, 79–84, https://www.artforum.com/print/196706/paragraphs-on-conceptual-art-36719 [last accessed 13 July 2021].

1. Minimal

MINIMAL has become a common term, used especially in the field of design and art in a wide range of areas such as fashion, music, dance, fine arts, design, architecture and literature, as well as regarding ornaments.

MINIMAL is generally viewed as an art achievement of the 1960s. From a purely formal perspective, it appeared as early as the 1920s. At that time it was not associated with ornament, which had recently lost its acceptance. Puristic striped, rectangular and triangular shapes emerged within the context of constructivist, Suprematist and concrete art.

If we look farther back, a similarly reduced form language already existed in the early period of advanced cultures such as in China and Egypt (4000–2000 BCE) and earlier in Magdalenia (ca. 10,000 BCE). However, even earlier in the Aurignacian (ca. 40,000 BCE), whose animal and hunting images represent a turning point, ornamental incisions with strictly reduced geometric shapes have been found on rocks alongside naturalistic paintings. In South Africa, in the Blombos cave near Cape Town, minimalist geometric forms including stripes, rectangles and triangles have been found starting in 1991, usually on ostrich eggshells. They are mostly linearly scored, and less often have colored surfaces and dots. They confirm that as early as roughly 70,000 BCE there was already a minimalist geometric form language.

Doesn't this justify any suspicions that such minimalist vocabulary is an anthropological constant that continues to surface? If the same basics take effect again and again, and all ornamental forms can be traced back to them, it seems natural to use this as the basis for developing a new ornament theory.

FREE with DOTS, Pattern with circles based on a Japanese model

FREE with LINES, Interrupted endless SINE WAVES

FREE with LINES, Double lines

21   FREE with PLANES, Triangular planes, Pointed ends

FREE with PLANES, Triangular planes, Rounded

FREE with DOTS, Large dots

STRIPED with DOTS

STRIPED with LINES, Wavy lines

STRIPED with LINES, Diagonal

STRIPED with DOTS

STRIPED with PLANES

STRIPED with LINES, Based on a Chinese model

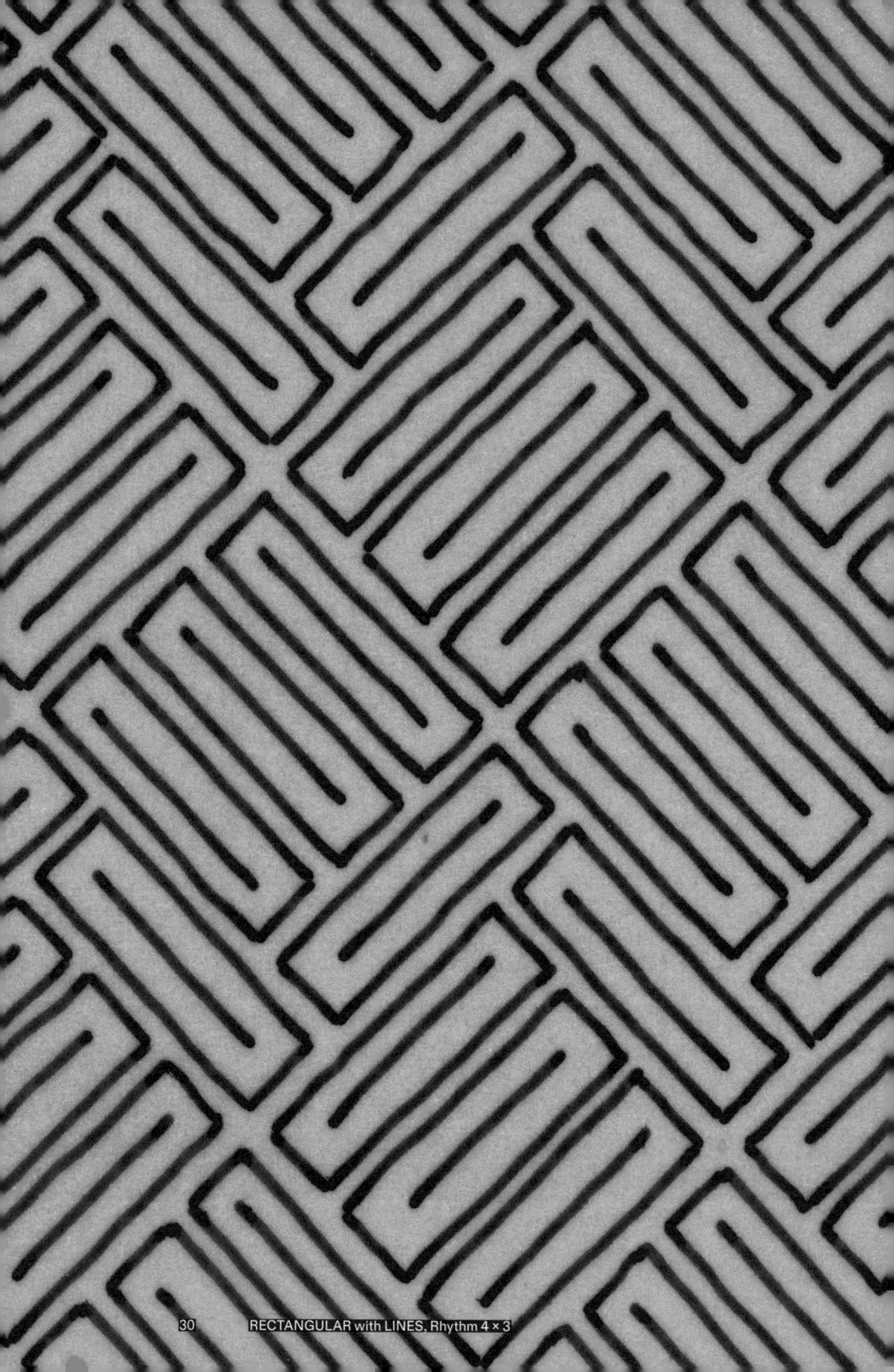

RECTANGULAR with LINES, Rhythm 4 × 3

RECTANGULAR with DOTS

RECTANGULAR with LINES, Freestyle

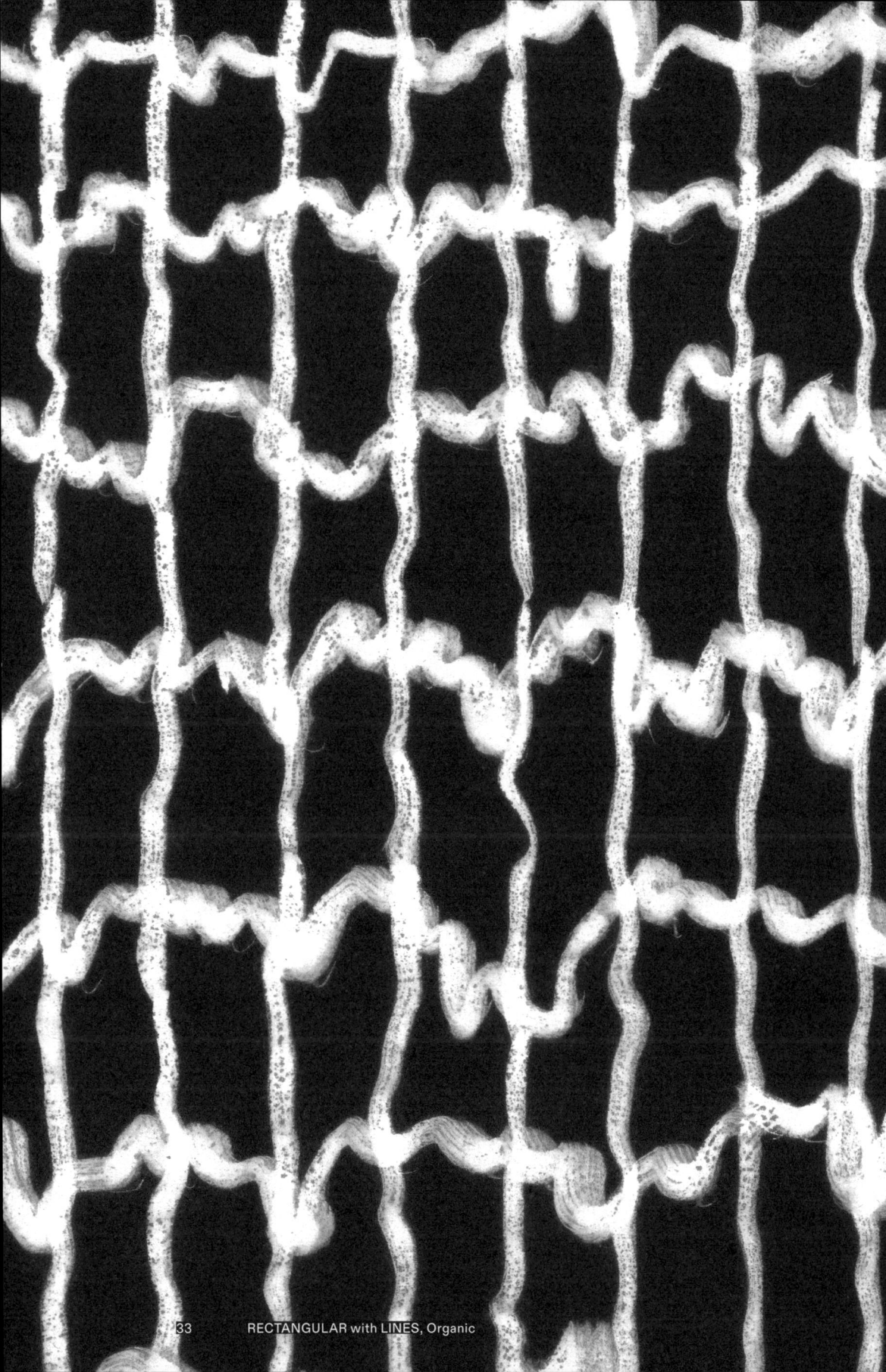

RECTANGULAR with LINES, Organic

RECTANGULAR with PLANES, Regular on a European model

TRIANGULAR with DOTS, Regular

TRIANGULAR with PLANES, Regular

TRIANGULAR with LINES, Regular/Irregular

TRIANGULAR with LINES, Regular grid, Irregular filled with SINE WAVES

TRIANGULAR with DOTS

1. Minimal
1.1 Free

MINIMAL: FREE is today the most popular ornamental concept. At first glance at least, it seems to follow no order at all. Whereas the arrangement principles of STRIPED, RECTANGULAR and TRIANGULAR are clearly ordered, the FREE principle gives the impression that the shapes that go together are joined arbitrarily and at most according to aesthetic aspects. And yet, like the other ornamental systems of arrangement in which shapes are arranged according to a strictly specified system, the FREE category does also have to do with order.

The FREE category, namely, describes a visual phenomenon: The same or similar shapes, apparently randomly scattered and without any ordering system, give the impression of an ornamental order that results through the similarity of the shapes. If that were not the case, then one would only get an impression of chaos and randomness. Three photos from everyday life shall serve to illustrate this: tapioca pearls, rafted timber and a cross-section of a piece of styrofoam.

| 1.1.1 | with Dots
Tapioca pearls | 1.1.2 | with Lines
Rafted timber | 1.1.3 | with Planes
Cross-section styrofoam block |

  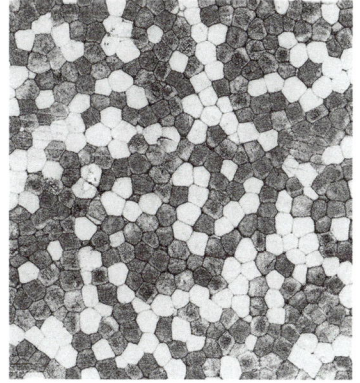

1.1.1 Minimal Free with Dots

The arrangements initially seem simple, but they show many different variants of MINIMAL: FREE with DOTS, that is, varied sizes, varied spacing, ring-shaped or solid, dark on a light background or light on a dark background, circular or oval, two- or multi-colored, with or without patterning, the best-known form of which is arched or circular.

PRESENT
MINIMAL: FREE with DOTS is one of the most popular ornamental principles world-wide. The Japanese artist Yayoi Kusama became famous for her polka-dot art.

PAST
Past examples of this principle are temples on Malta whose exterior stone walls are covered with thousands of round depressions, Le Mas d'Azil cave in southern France, with countless dots painted on pebbles (ca. 9000 BCE), and the Blombos cave (ca. 70,000 BCE; see page 7).

1

2

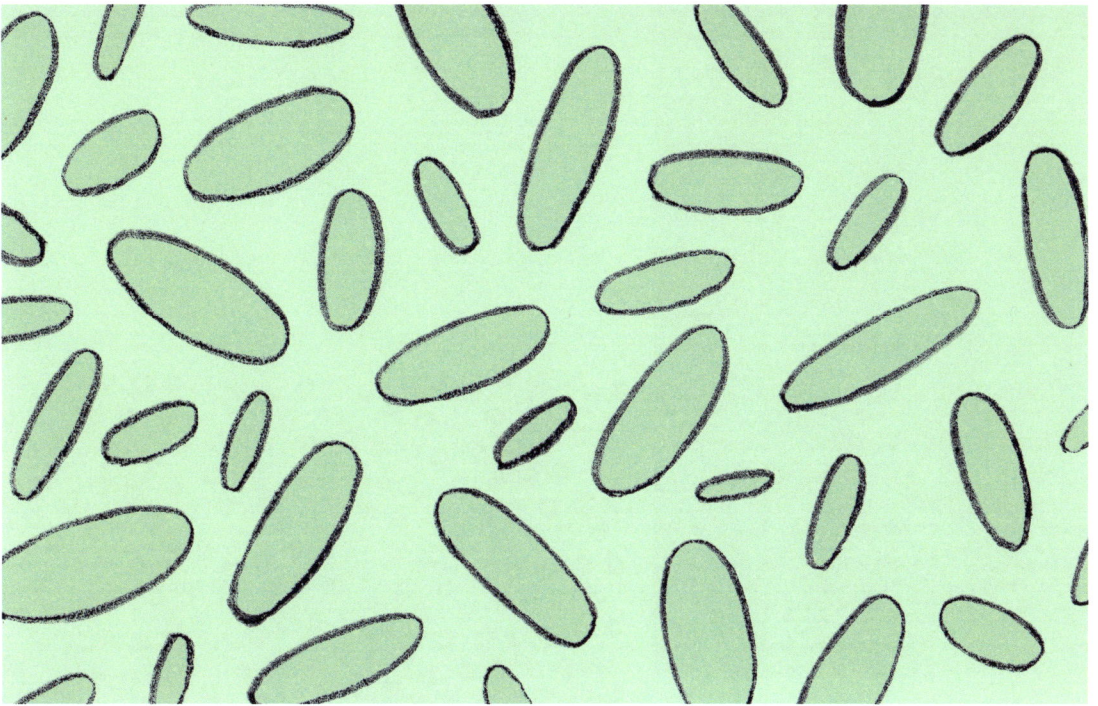

3

4

5

6

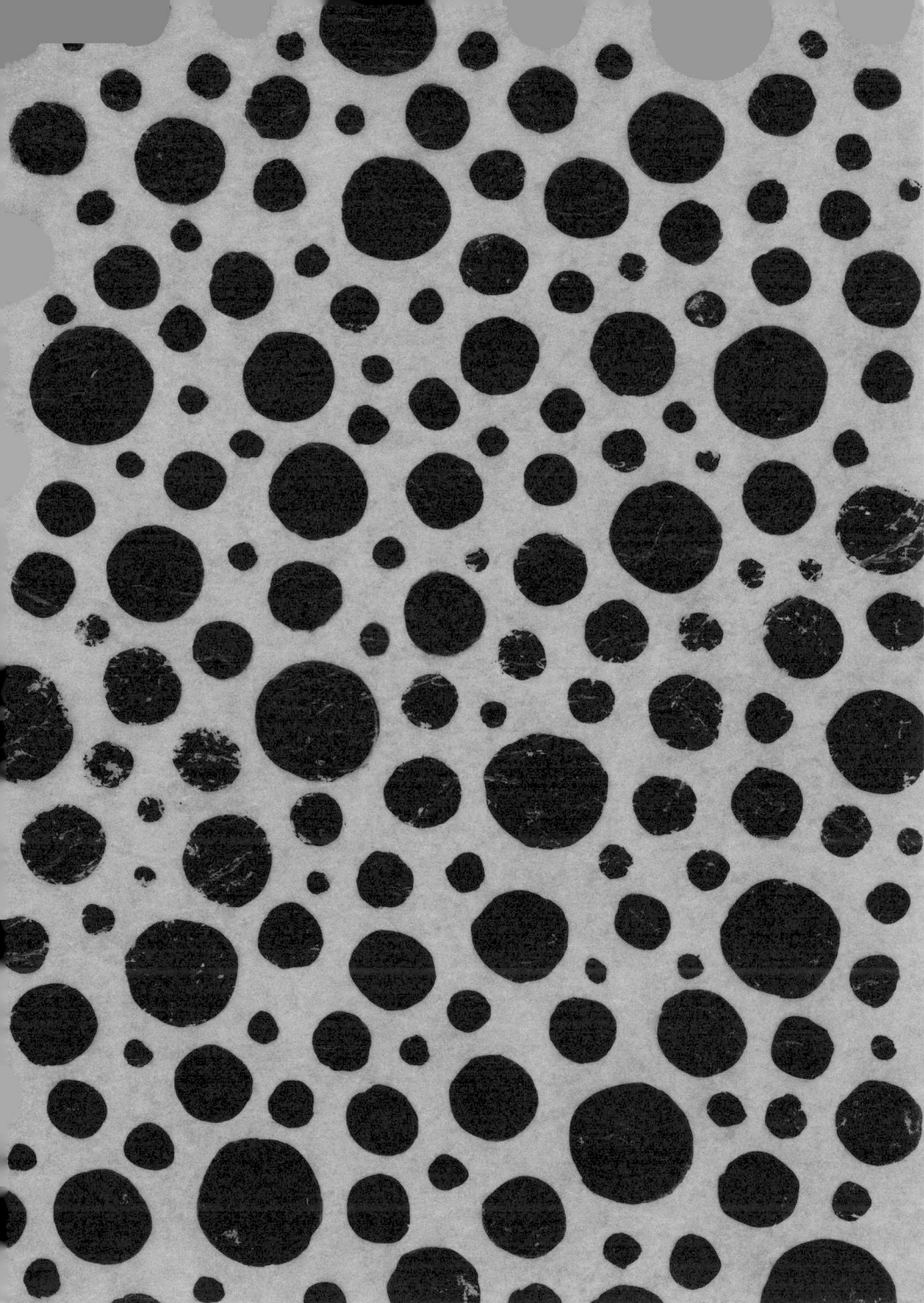

7

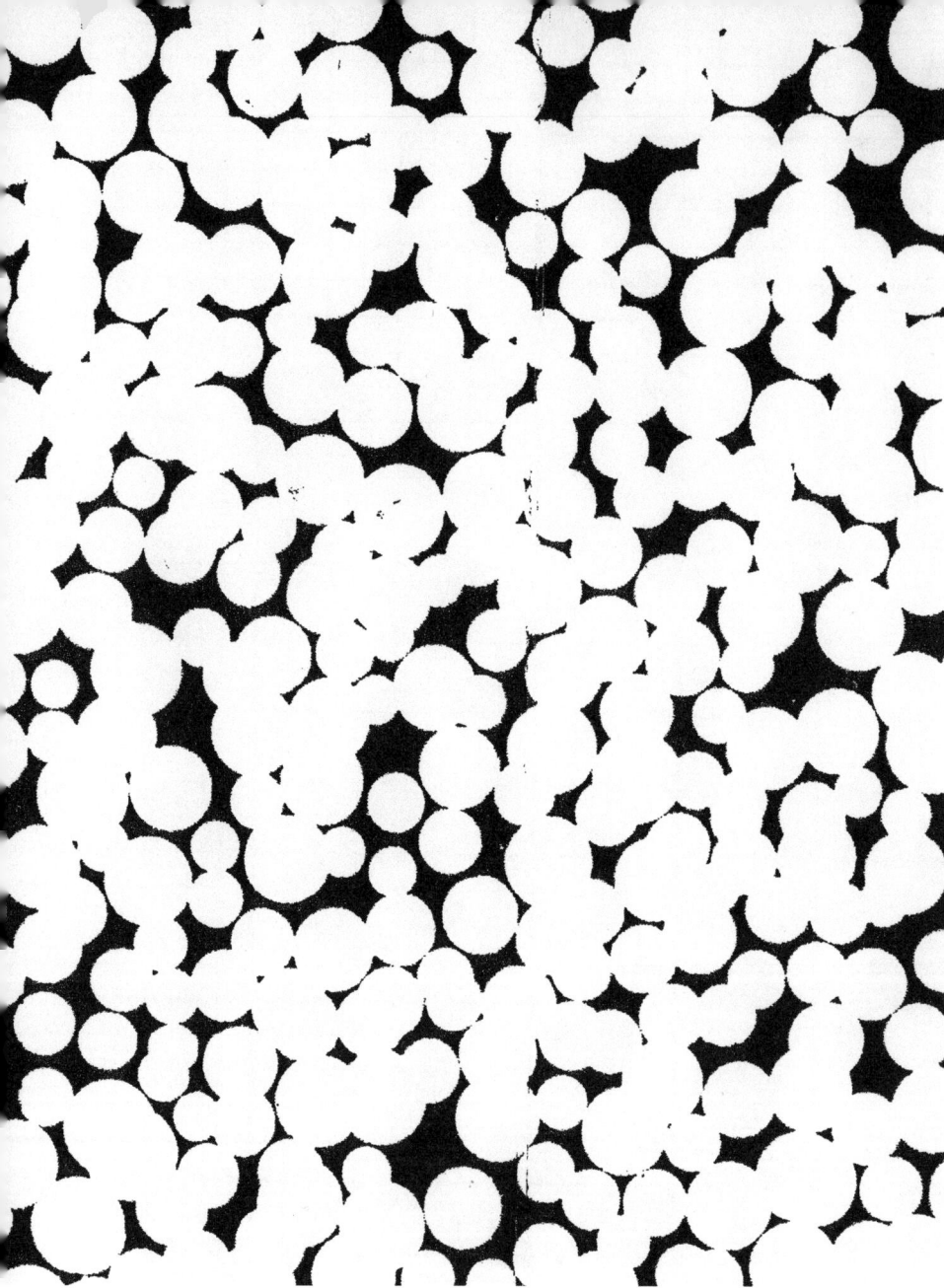

8

9

10

11

1.1.2 Minimal Free with Lines

The following lines are shown: interrupted endless lines, double lines, isolated scattered lines, angled and curved lines, tapered lines with and without a pronounced end-marking, cellular or Y-shaped forms.

PRESENT
Visually familiar as straws following the harvest, drinking straws sliding out of the package, Mikado (pick-up) sticks on the table, logs floating in the water.

PAST
FREE with LINES principle was predominantly used on textiles and ceramic vessels in Japan.

1

2

4

3

5

6

7

8

9

1   Simple lines with wide spacing, MINIMAL version
2   Angled lines with patterning
3   Y-shaped (3-pointed star) with close spacing

4   Craquelé (crackled)
5   Curved lines with close spacing
6   Curved lines, tapered shape

7   Angled form with close spacing
8   Double lines with close spacing
9   Curved line with pronounced end-marking

1.1.3 Minimal Free with Planes

Object-free[3] shapes with one to five pointed vertices will be systematically shown; with straight, convex, concave or organic borders. The pentagram and craquelé offer forms with tessellation.

PRESENT
MINIMAL: FREE with PLANES is the most popular ornamental principle for figurative shapes, such as animals and humans, which, however, go beyond the scope of the present book. A cross-section of a styrofoam block is an example of object-free planes in a free order; irregular pentagonal planes surprisingly form a balanced composition.

PAST
The architect Antoni Gaudi covered entire interior shells with craquelé (crackled patterns).

1

2

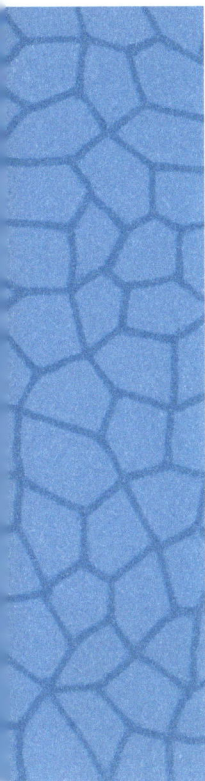

3

3   See translator's note on p. 332.

3

4

5

6

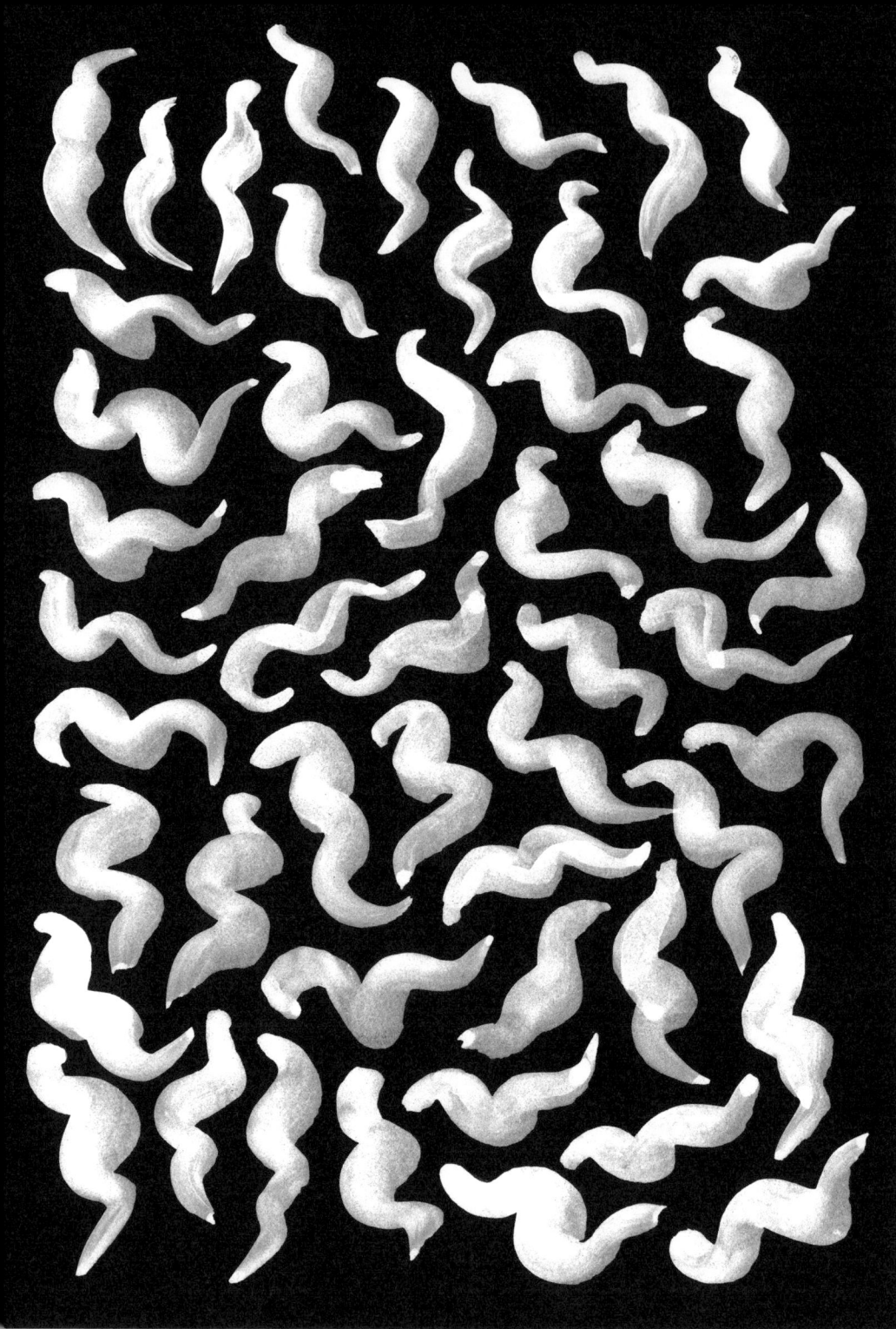

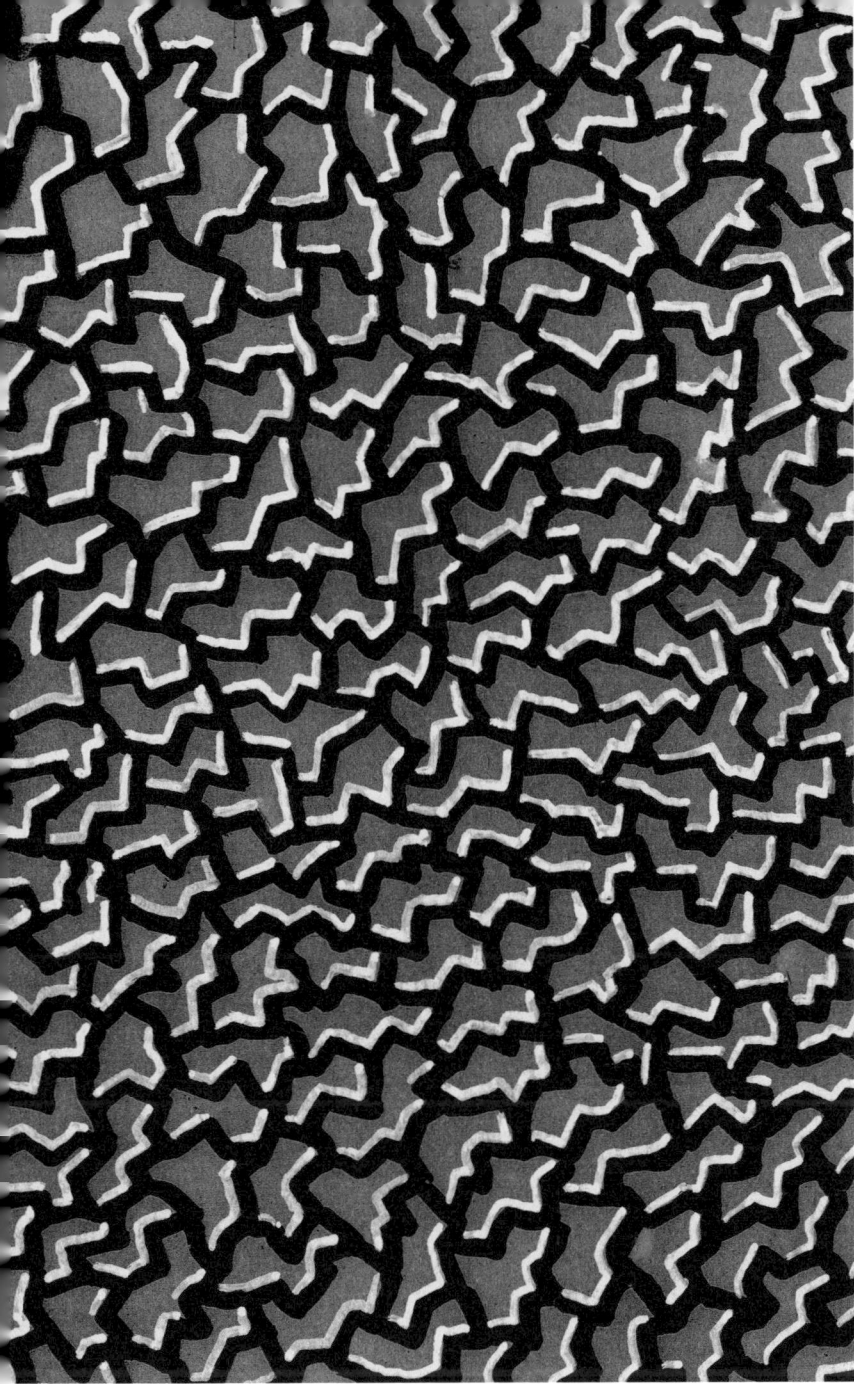

8

9

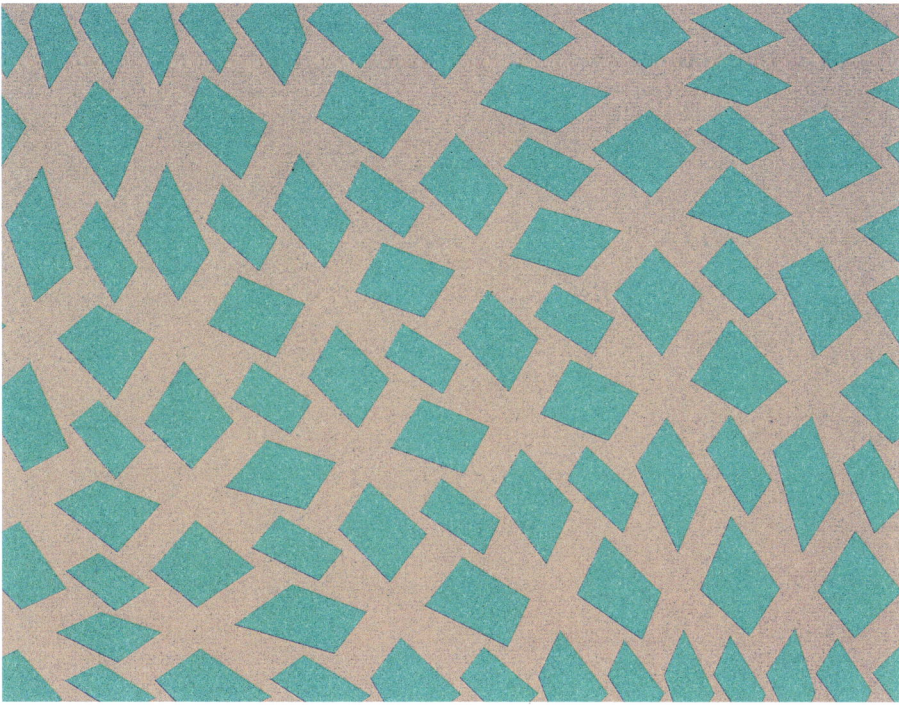

10

1. Minimal
1.2 Striped

Deliberate execution of a straight line in prehistoric times is probably the most significant creative act in the history of art that is free of any representational figures. This then led to striped, rectangular or triangular ornamental arrangements of this line. Even today, quickly sketched lines and conceptual sketches subconsciously link us to this fundamental act of creation. In times when things are viewed predominantly as representations, straight lines are readily seen as an abstraction of the horizon. The surroundings such as in Blombos Cave, however, show that parallel lines and crossed lines in a rectangle or triangle are not the image of anything, but instead come from an object-free imagination.

It was of course a long way from these first lines to the precise parallel stripes on the American flag or from the first threads spanned between two wooden blocks on a simple loom to modern textiles. It is perhaps due to the familiarity with textiles going far back in history that STRIPES are today still one of the most popular ornamental arrangements. The greatest triumph of this concept, however, can be found in the use of all sorts of script. In the form of lines it forms the basis from which all letters and graphic characters gain context and meaning. The principle of STRIPES has provided the form for script, whether horizontally from left to right as in the West, from right to left in the Middle East, or from top to bottom in much of the Far East.

1.2.1   with Dots
Korean letters

1.2.2   with Lines
Print by Günter Fruhtrunk

1.2.3   with Planes
Brick wall

1.2.1 Minimal Striped with Dots

Round, oval, triangular and rectangular dots are arranged in straight or curved rows, directly touching or following lines, or enclosed within lines.

PRESENT
MINIMAL: STRIPED with DOTS principle constitutes the basis for everything that is read in the form of letters and characters – horizontal as in Europe and the Middle East, and vertical in major parts of the Far East.

PAST
The first known example of MINIMAL: STRIPED with DOTS is in the form of shells strung on threads in South Africa; this arrangement was later found in painted rows on stones. (Swabian Jura 40,000 BCE, see page 8)

1

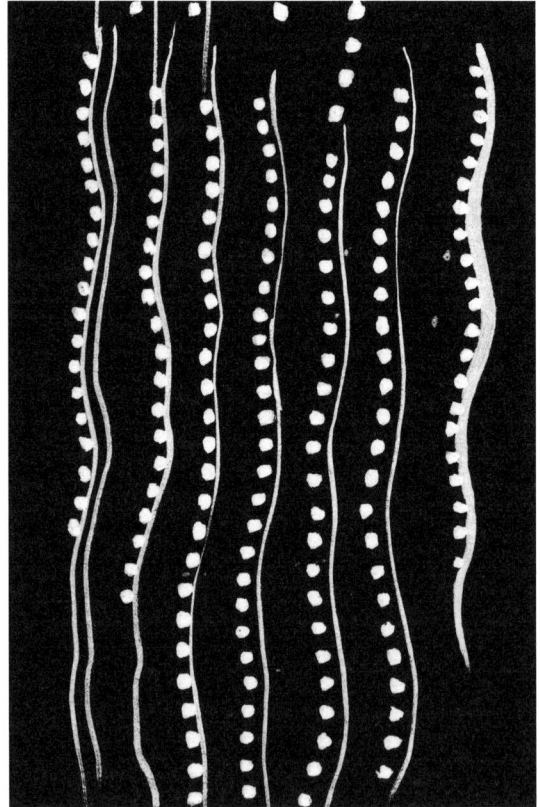

2

3

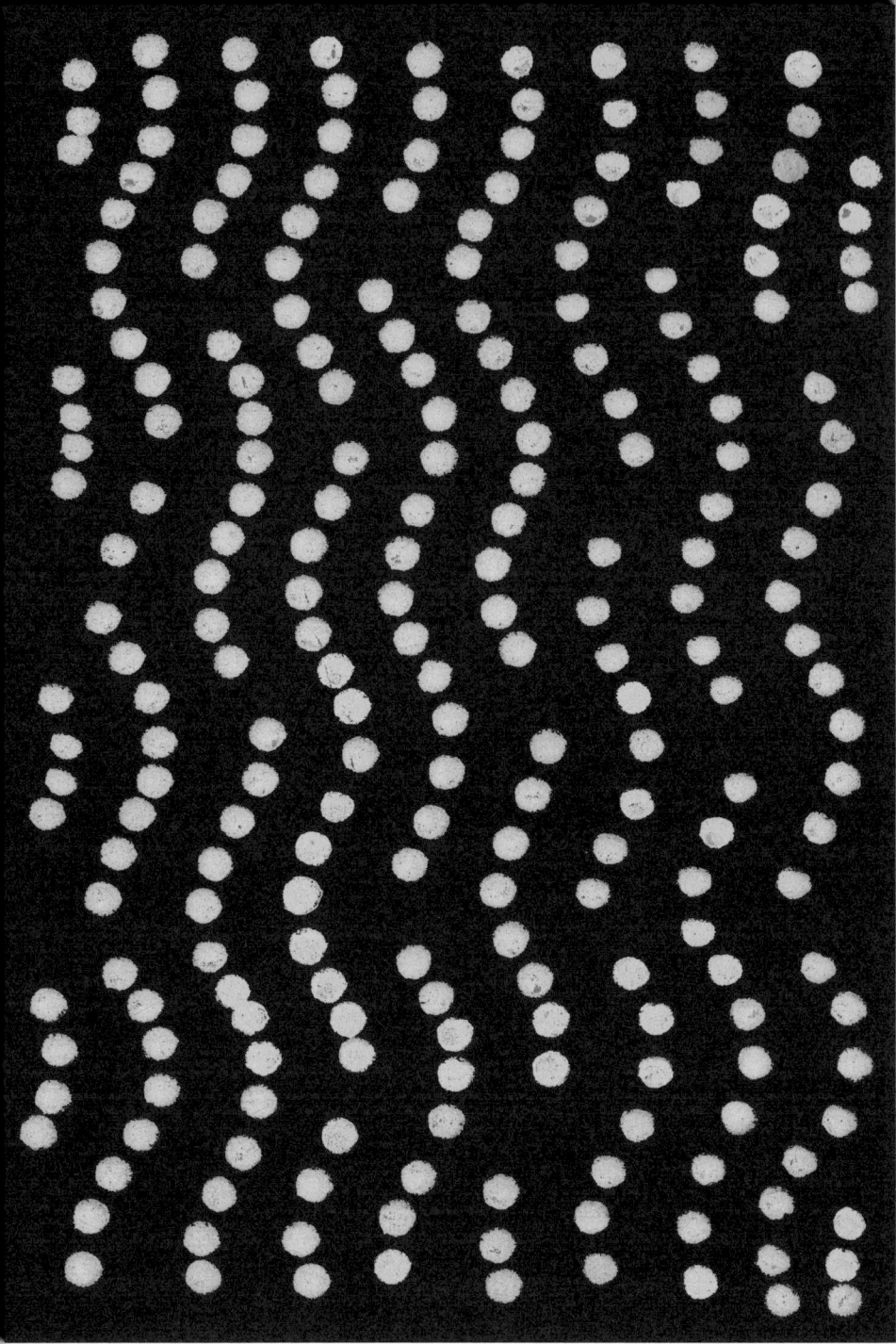

4

5

6

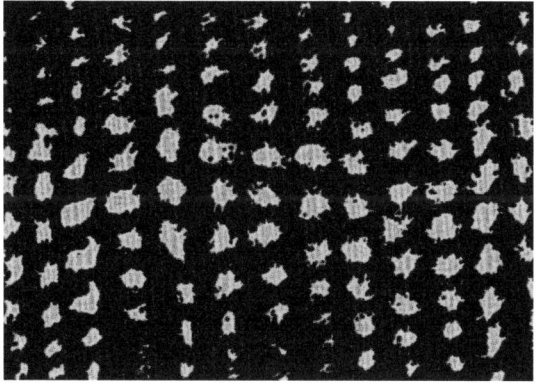

7

8

9

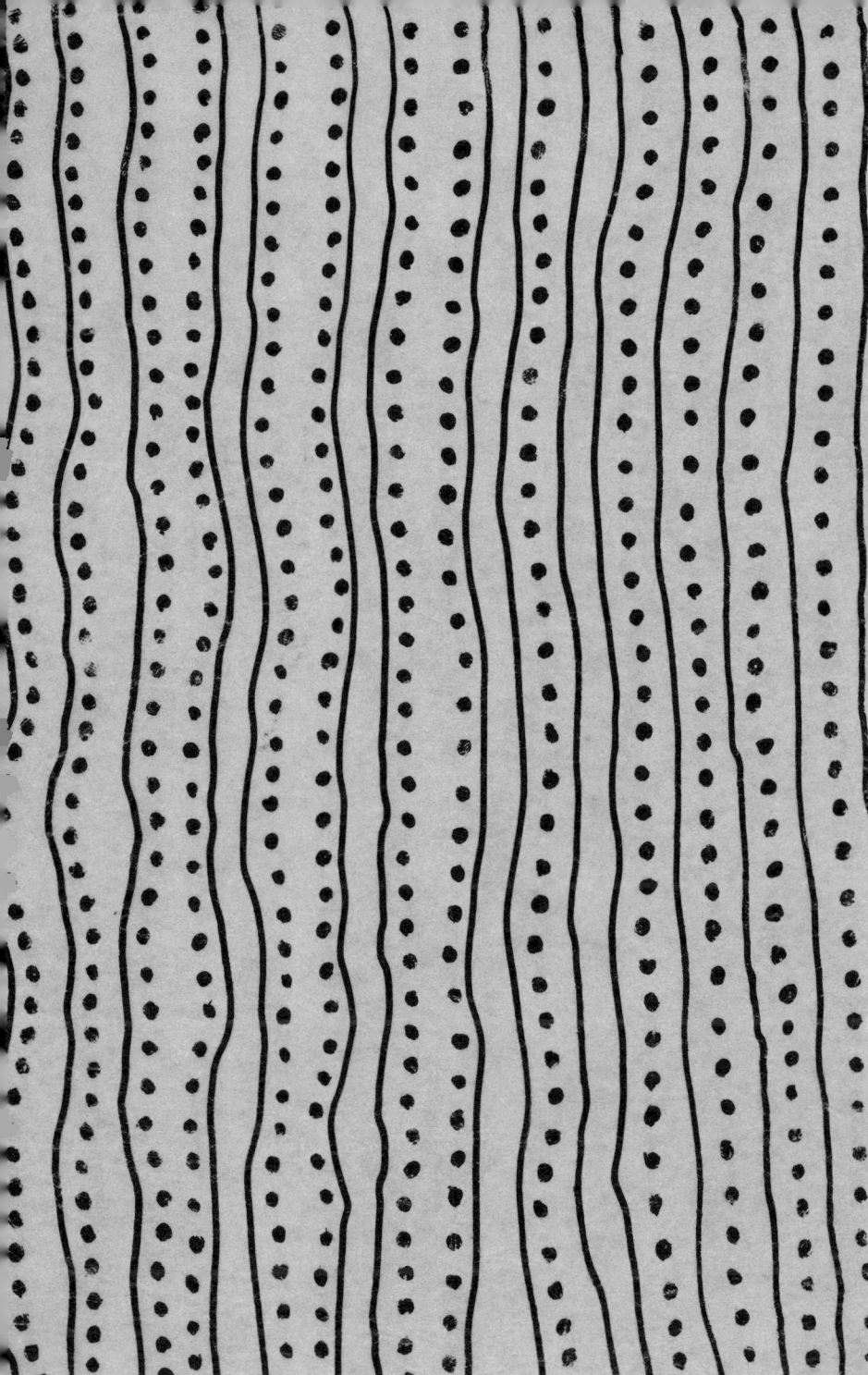

1.2.2 Minimal Striped with Lines

From the abundance of possibilities, straight and wavy lines are shown, as are continuous and interrupted, organic and geometric, rhythmic and deliberately disrupted.

PRESENT
Every roof with rows of roof shingles and all kinds of slatted blinds as a shade to block out light or heat displays the MINIMAL: STRIPED with LINES ornamental principle.

PAST
Horizontal timbers were used in house construction; cities and fortresses were surrounded by vertical stakes (palisades).

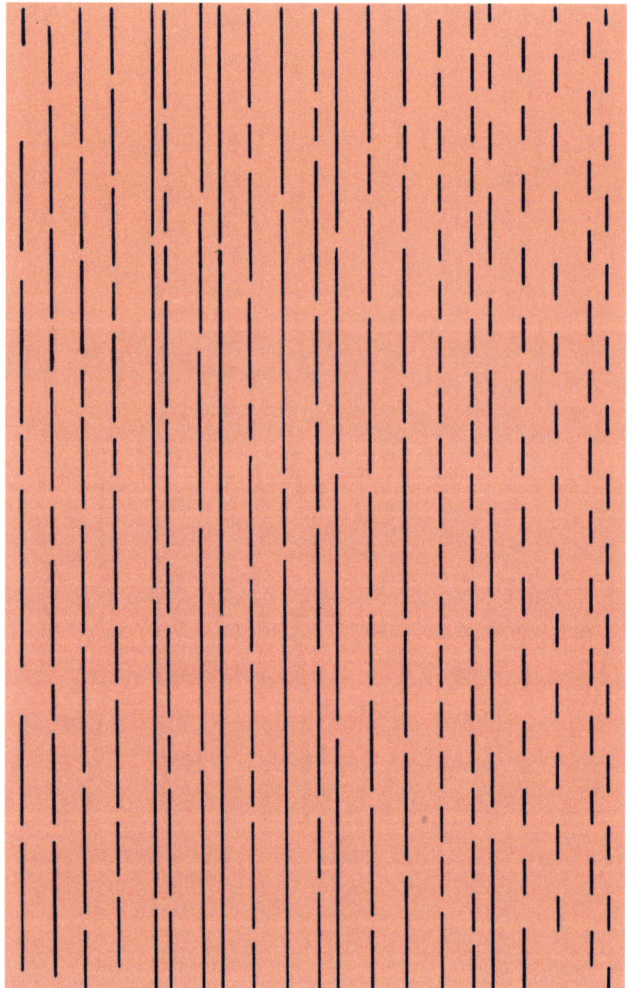

1

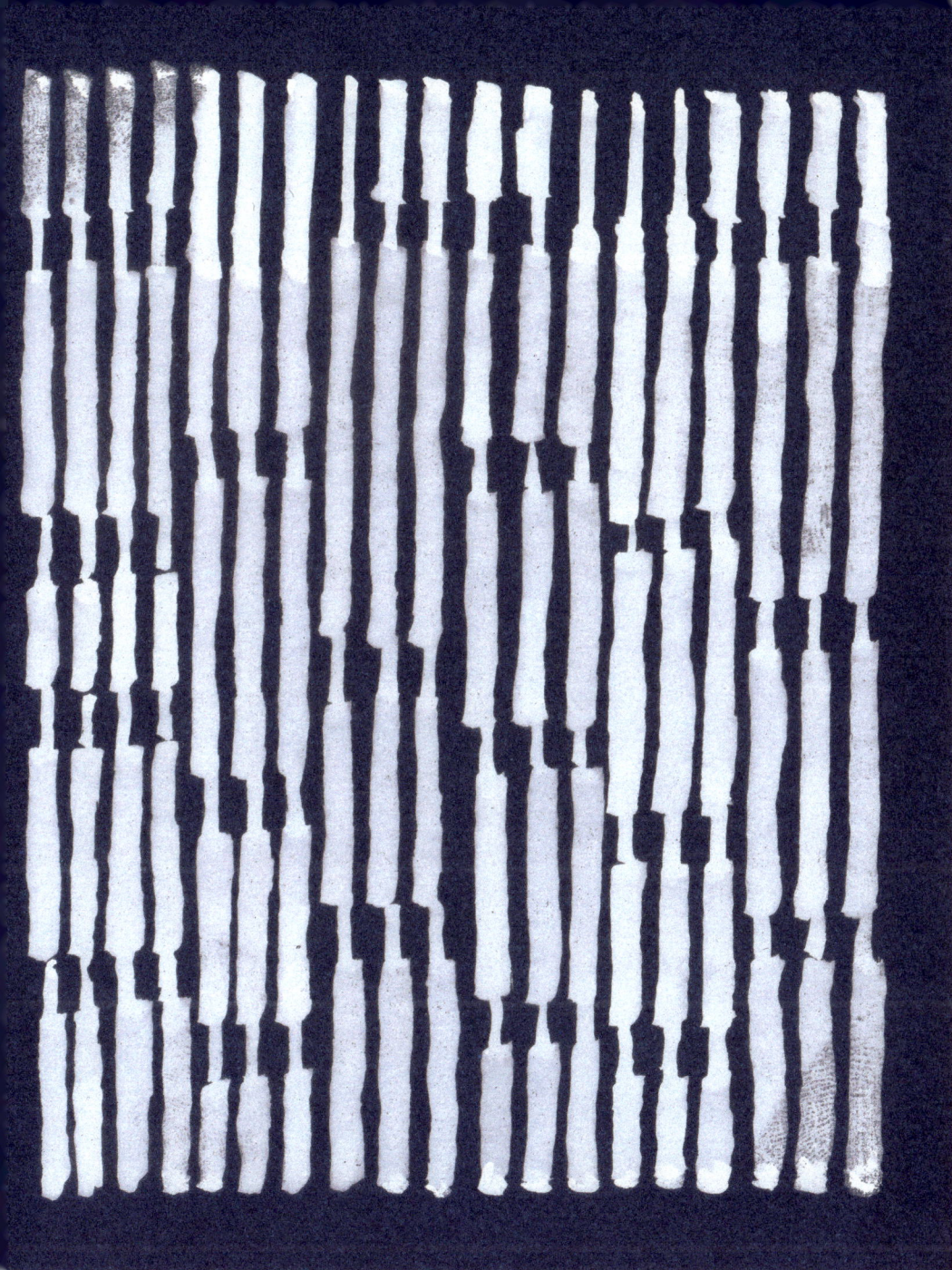

2

3

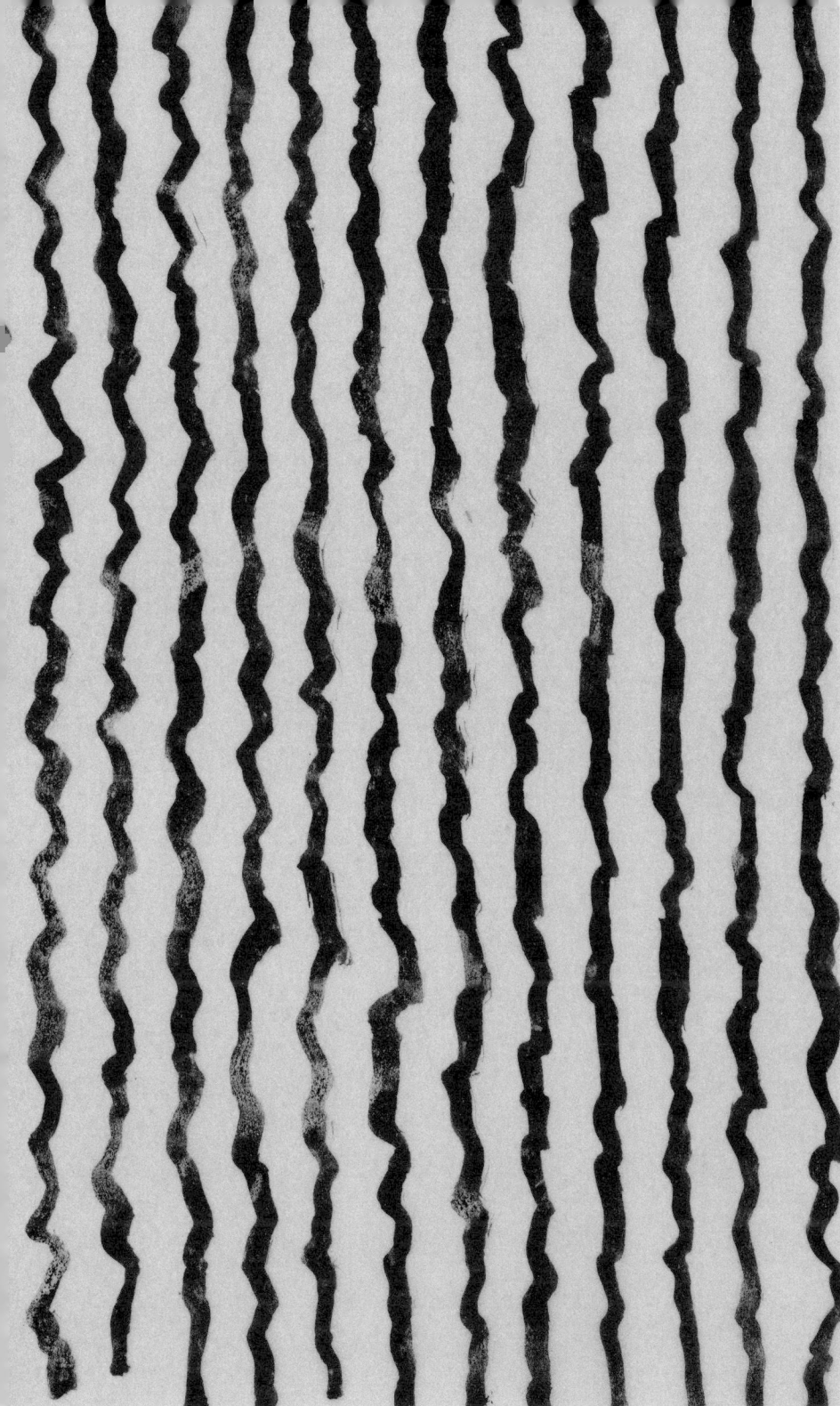

4

5

6

Lines

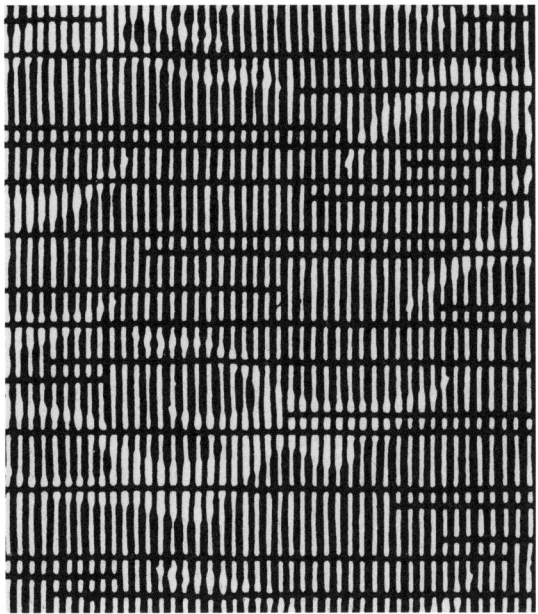

7

8

9

10

11

12

1 MINIMAL version
2 Rhythmic shift
3 Organic rhythm
4 Organic rhythm

5 Disrupted double line on a European model
6 Wavy lines
7 Two rhythms based on a Japanese model
8 Interrupted wavy lines

9 Organic interruption
10 Asymmetric interruption
11 Fishbone double line
12 Parallel lines based on a Japanese model

1.2.3 Minimal Striped with Planes

2

The planar shift to oblong rectangles, sometimes in a light-dark contrast and sometimes tipped to diagonals, is an example of this principle being used for aesthetically pleasing solutions.

PRESENT
All exposed brickwork, with its horizontal mortar joints and rectangular brick surfaces, is based on the MINIMAL: STRIPED with PLANES ornamental principle. High-rise buildings show that this concept is also suitable to emphasize the vertical.

PAST
This arrangement has been used for millennia in the form of horizontal clay bricks, representing the genesis of all architecture.

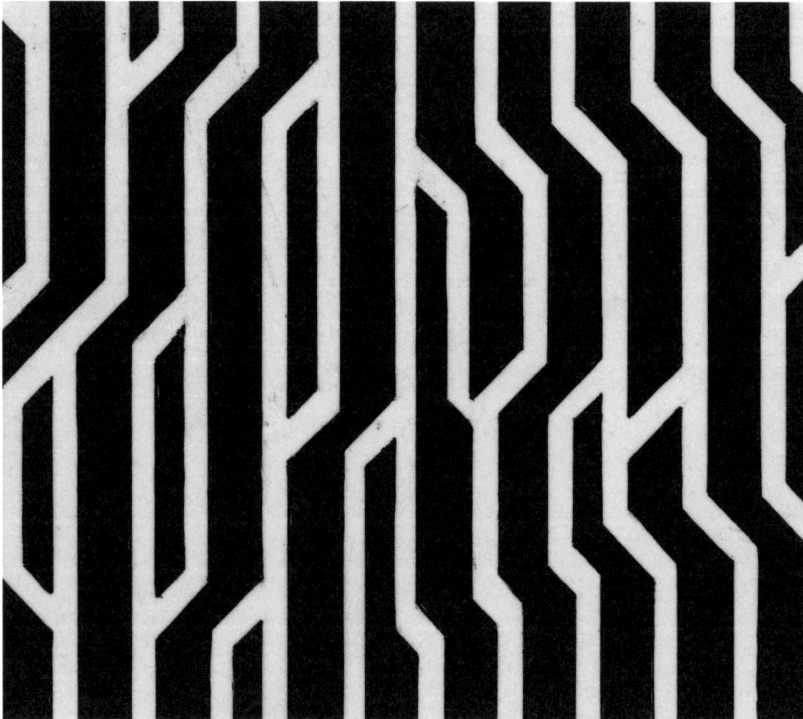

1

3

4

5

6

7

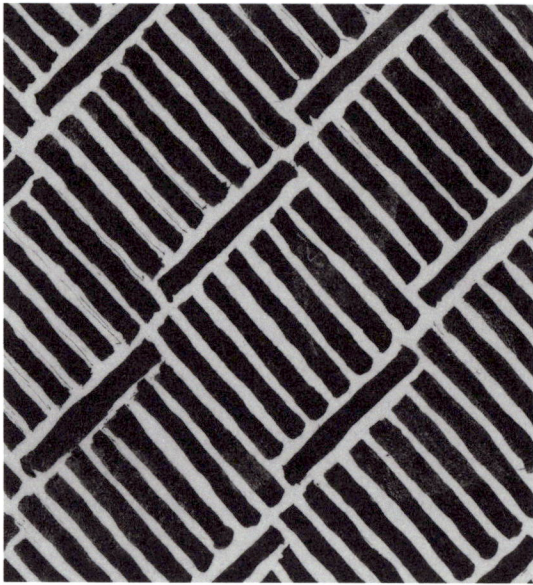

8

9

10

1. Minimal
1.3 Rectangular

Here we immediately find an example by looking at a smart phone or laptop, which is only possible because of the established routine of using the MINIMAL: RECTANGULAR simple ornamental principle. It is the perfect ordering system for shapes that can be shifted to the left and right as well as upward and downward. Spatially, this system also pertains to the dimensions forward and backward. When the inhabitants of Cape Town etched the first rectangles 70,000 years ago, were they thinking of architecture or smart phones? Or did they depict something having a related form in their environment, such as salt or rare pyrite or fluorspar crystals? Certainly not. But it is conceivable that these were representations of positive feelings of being a part of the universe, as they sometimes appear in dreams of mandalas. Prerequisite for the presentation of a rectangle was the discovery of the straight line, as described in MINIMAL: STRIPED (page 64). At that time people surely did not imagine the future of MINIMAL: RECTANGULAR yet to come. But they "anchored" the rectangle in their genes, and used it to build the first settlements around 10,000 BCE. The fact that this ornamental concept would be used to develop the entire built environment, extending all the way to data processing, lets us view the small ostrich egg shards from Cape Town with a certain awe.

1.3.1   with Dots
Metal sheet

1.3.2   with Lines
Plexiglas roof of the Olympic
Arena in Munich

1.3.3   with Planes
Metal grid, partly filled with
snow

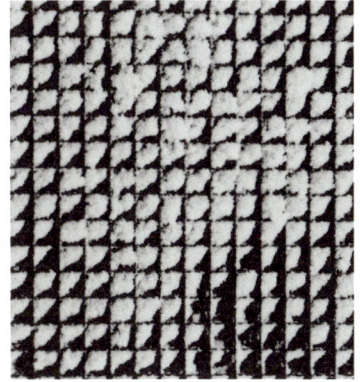

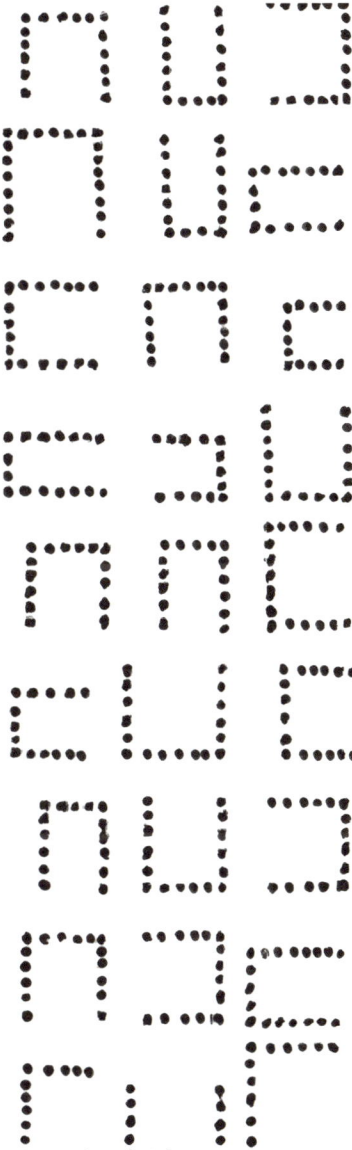

1.3.1 Minimal Rectangular with Dots

Various systems with square or round dots are depicted freely or precisely. The design intention is to develop a playful view of a formal arrangement that appears at first glance to be indestructible.

PRESENT
The invention and use of smart phones and computers is a result of the MINIMAL: RECTANGULAR with DOTS arrangement principle that is inherent to human beings. Every command is entered by pressing a square button.

PAST
For technological reasons, small windows used to be built, forming a so-called punched-window façade as viewed from the outside. They can be considered the visual precursor to present-day keyboards.

1

3

4

5

6

7

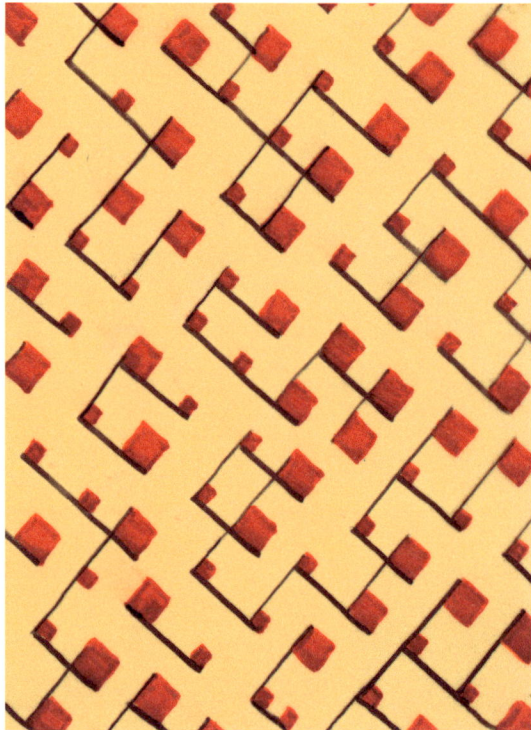

8

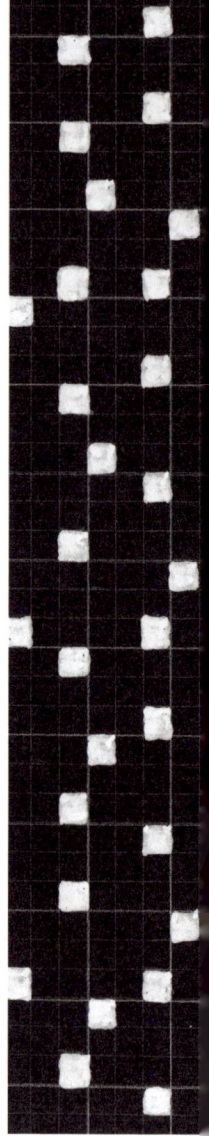

9

1   Square grid based on a Japanese model
2   MINIMAL version
3   Model print
4   Open DOTS based on a Japanese model

5   Round DOTS, some shifted on a European Model
6   Square in a square grid made up of four squares
7   Free and regular arrangements
8   Shift in a ratio of 4:3

9   Square in a square grid made up of nine squares

1.3.2 Minimal Rectangular with Lines

Six varieties of MINIMAL: RECTANGULAR with LINES have been developed from a square, and two others break out of the strict system, showing conceptual possibilities.

PRESENT
Graph paper is the simplest variant of MINIMAL: RECTANGULAR with LINES, as is our clothing that is woven with warp and woof.

PAST
With few exceptions, construction has been based on plans with a right-angled linear framework, drawn in the ground or the sand and later sketched on papyrus.

1

2

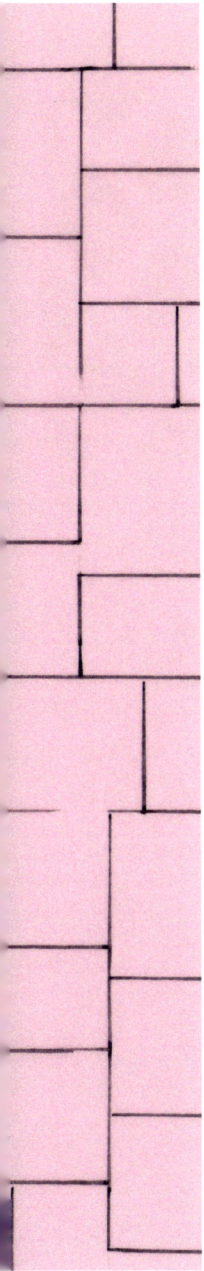

3

4

5

6

7

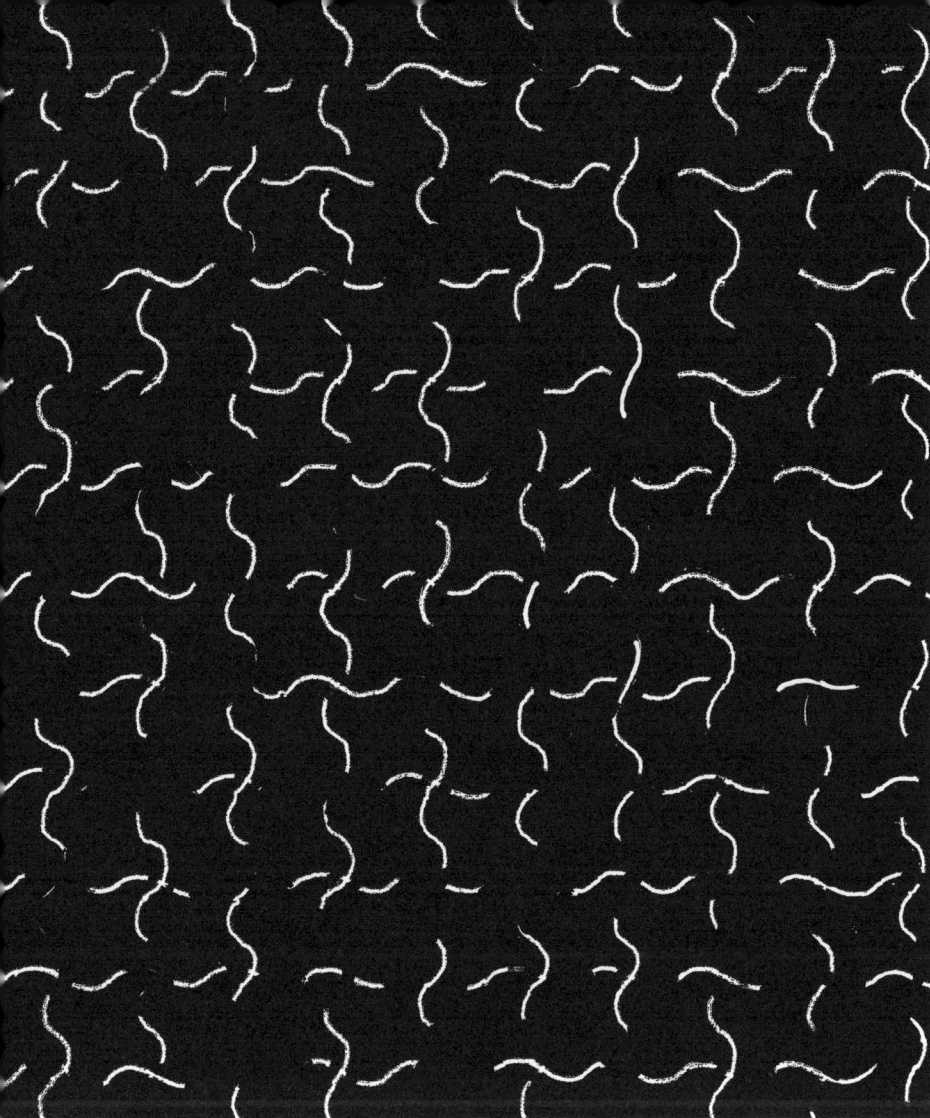

8

1.3.3 Minimal Rectangular with Planes

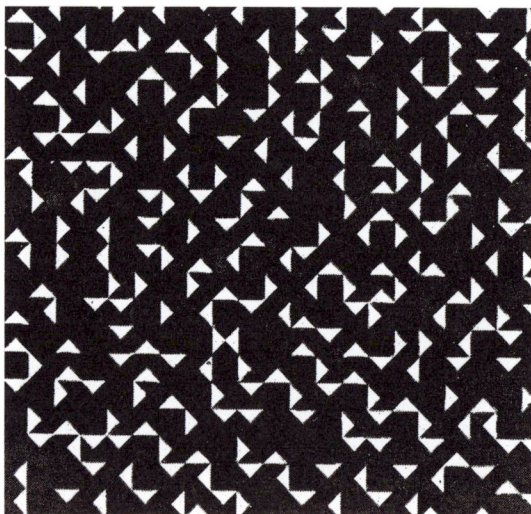

1

Light-dark, checkerboard-like variants are run through with right angles and diagonals in four geometrically precise versions and seven free ones.

PRESENT
Every modern building works with the MINIMAL: RECTANGULAR with PLANES ornamental principle: Exterior wall and façade elements, and interior tiles, floors, and ceiling elements.

PAST
In construction, the need for rectangular, planar elements for ceiling, walls, and floors was always great. The right angle was the best option in securing a trouble-free transition from one craft to the next.

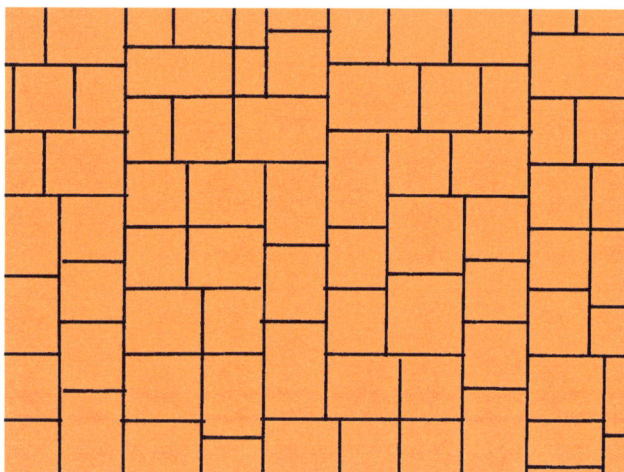

2

3

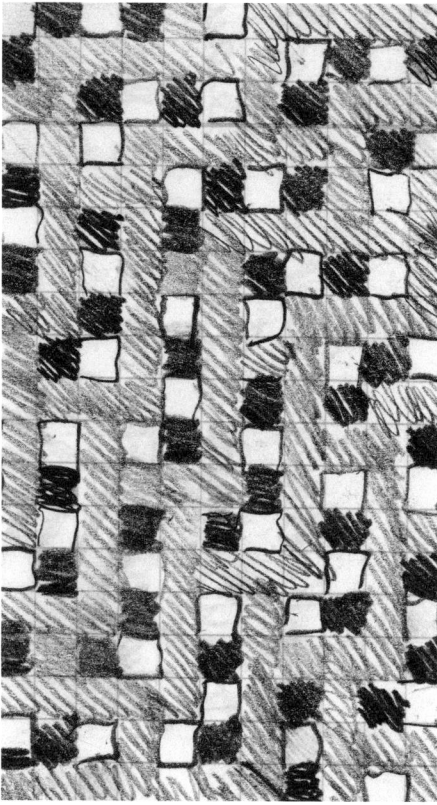

4

5

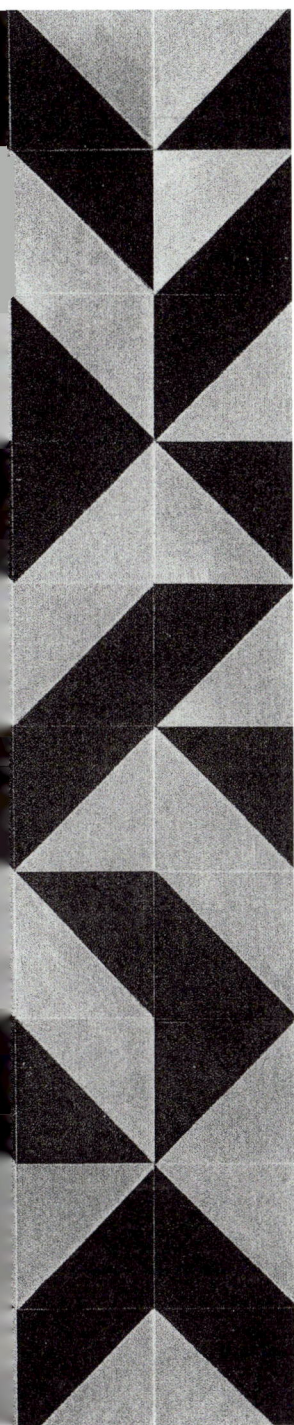

6

7

8

Planes

9

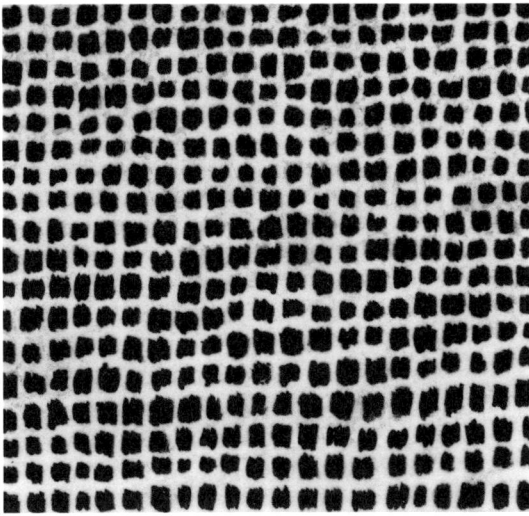

10

11

1. Minimal
1.4 Triangular

Today we find the triangle as a shape in connection with an ornamental arrangement in high voltage lattice towers, antennae, and when looking into wooden roof carpentry. Under an electron microscope, a triangular membrane around human cells can be seen as a biological variant of the TRIANGULAR principle. A triangular structure creates the most stable structure wherever light constructions are needed. But how did people 70,000 years ago discover such a form and an ornamental arrangement based on it? In contrast to RECTANGULAR, STRIPED, and POLKA-DOTTED ornamental arrangements, which do not represent anything existing, in this case there are models. These include the female vulva triangle as well as simple A-frame roofs of branches stuck into the ground. Like MINIMAL RECTANGULAR (page 88), equilateral triangles appear in dreams, as signs of inner strength. The options – from the greatest possible constructive strength to the Trinity in the Christian faith – show the symbolic range of the equilateral triangle.

1.4.1   with Dots
         Drum washing machine

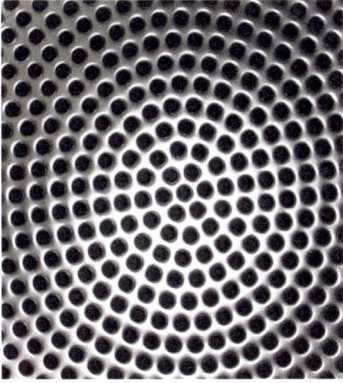

1.4.2   with Lines
         Reinforced geodesic dome,
         planetarium, Jena, Germany,
         1924

1.4.3   with Planes
         Spanish Pavilion by Foreign
         Office Architects, EXPO, Aichi,
         Japan, 2005

1.4.1 Minimal Triangular with Dots

Asymmetries are played with on the basis of strict grids: fat and thin DOTS, slight shifts, emphasis on the center of the DOT, halving DOTS, connecting triangles between two or three DOTS.

PRESENT
The most widespread form of MINIMAL: TRIANGULAR WITH DOTS can be found today in washing machines, coffee machines, and strainers – anywhere in which something is filtered, sifted, or aerated.

PAST
Tile facades made of clay were decorated with round cones of colored clay that were flush-mounted into the moist clay; metal and ceramic Roman household sieves were given functional grids of holes; large window grilles were hewn from marble for mosques.

1

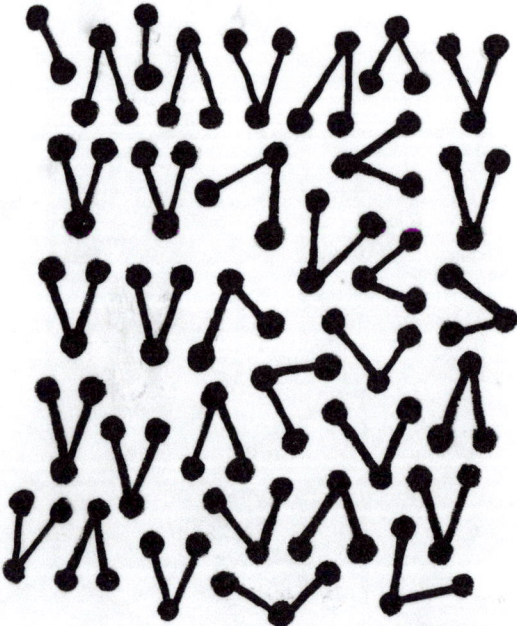

2

3

4

5

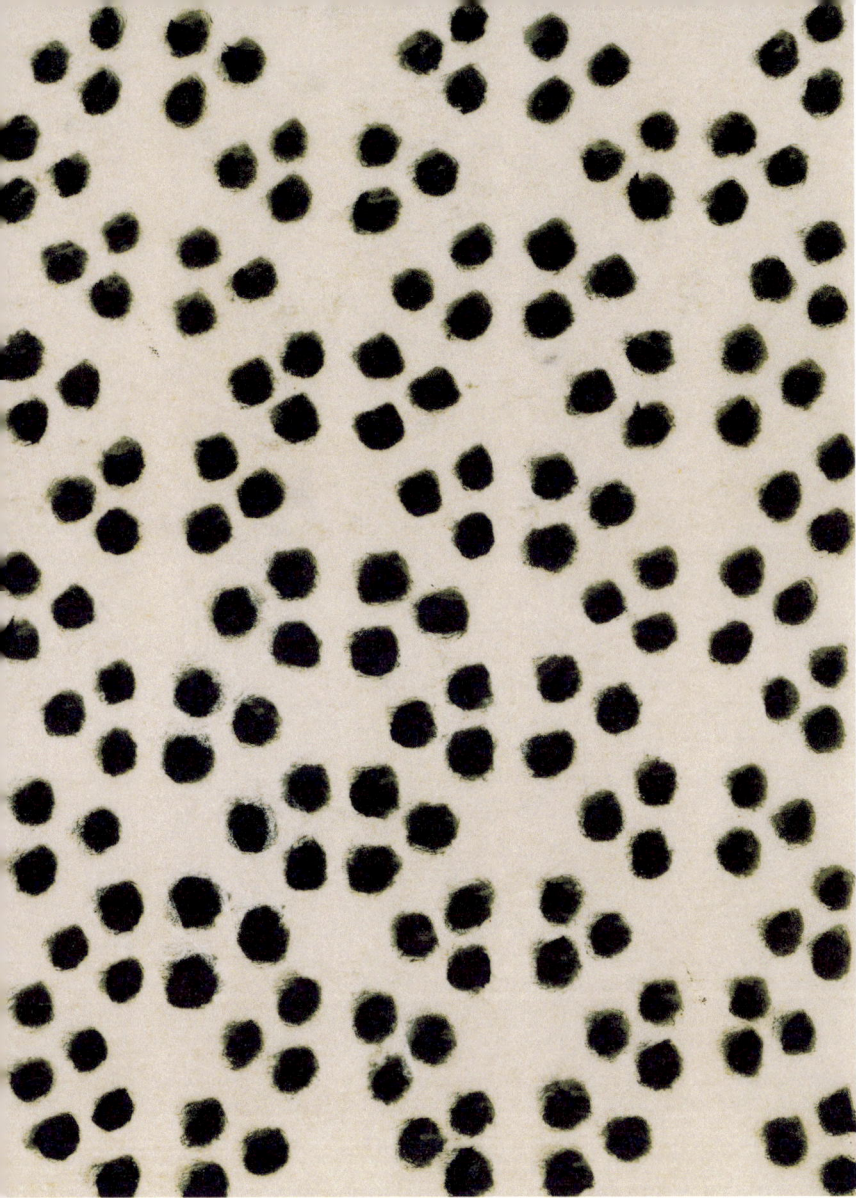

6

7

8

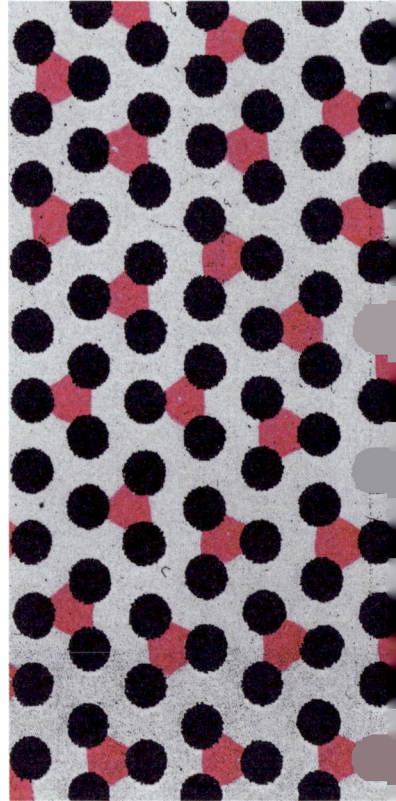

9

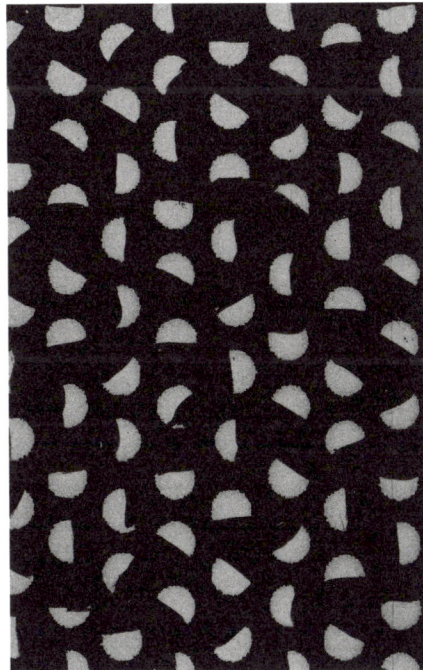

1.4.2 Minimal Triangular with Lines

A linear triangular grid continues to offer optical cohesiveness even when lines are omitted or interrupted. Its proximity to a hexagon (six triangles fill a hexagon) constantly introduces multiple readings between triangle and hexagon.

PRESENT
The most well-known linear image of MINIMAL: TRIANGULAR WITH LINES can be found in lattice towers, bridges, and glass domes. A triangle with fixed corner connections is the most stable constructive element in building.

PAST
Unsurpassed in diversity and design are wooden so-called ice-ray lattice windows in China and marble window grilles from Persia or northern India.

1

2

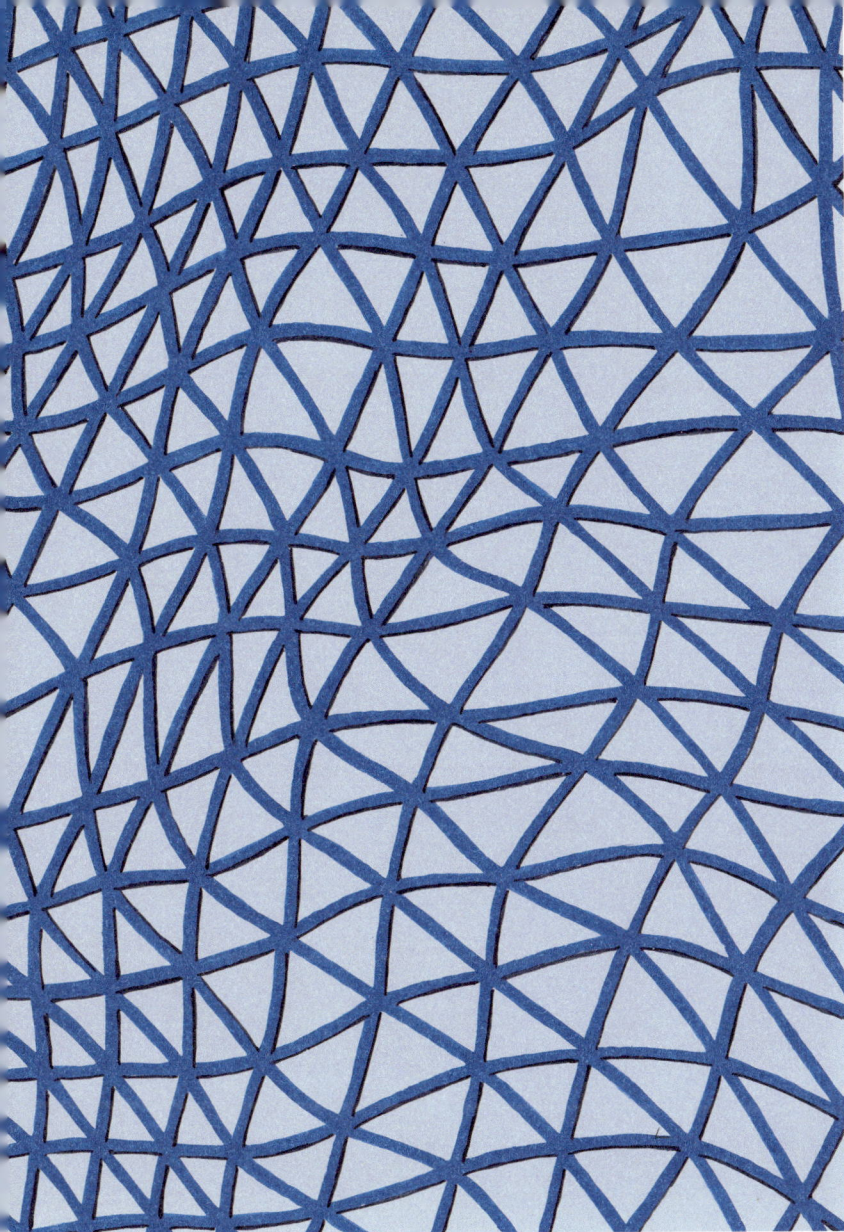

3

4

5

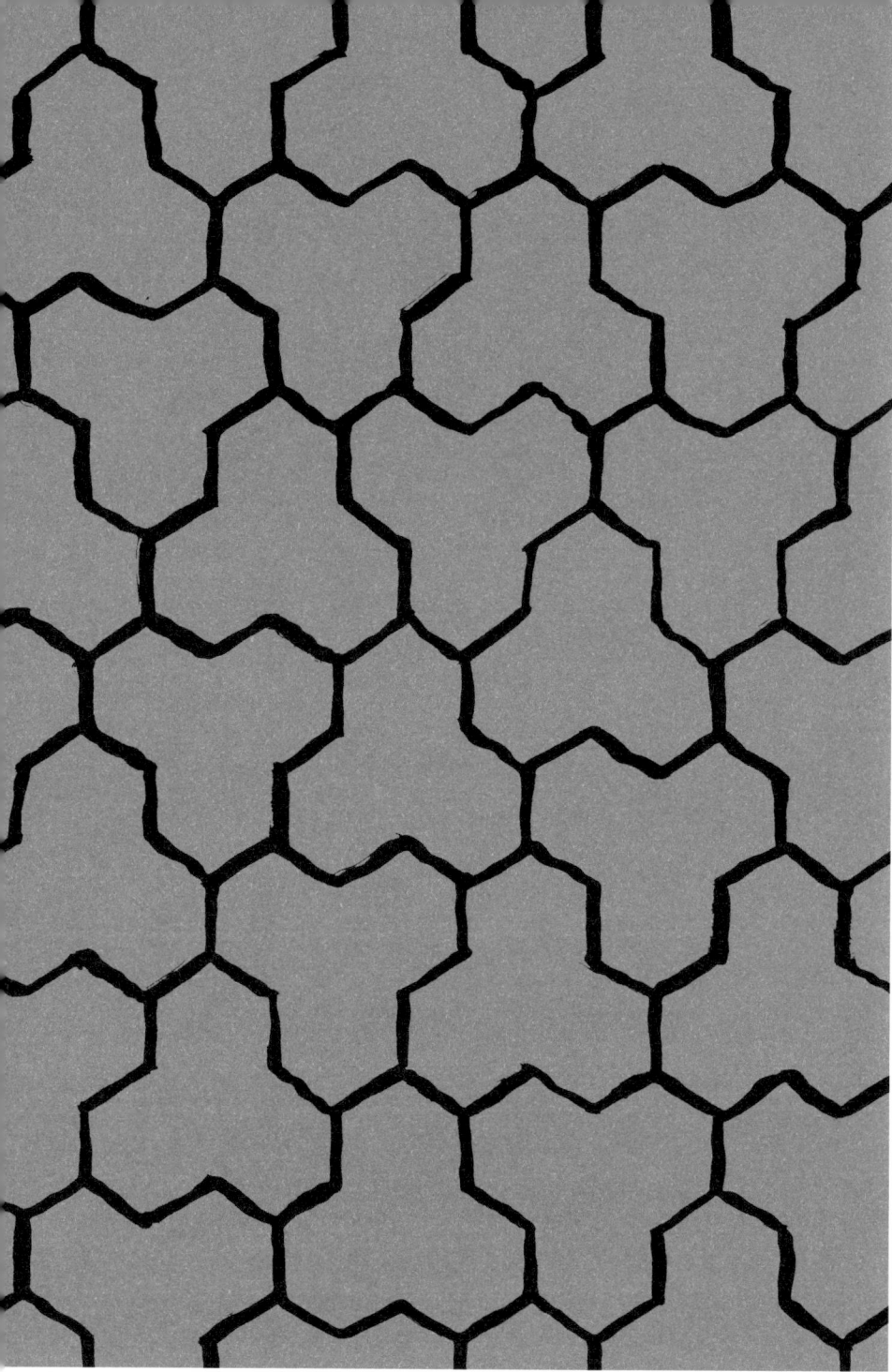

6

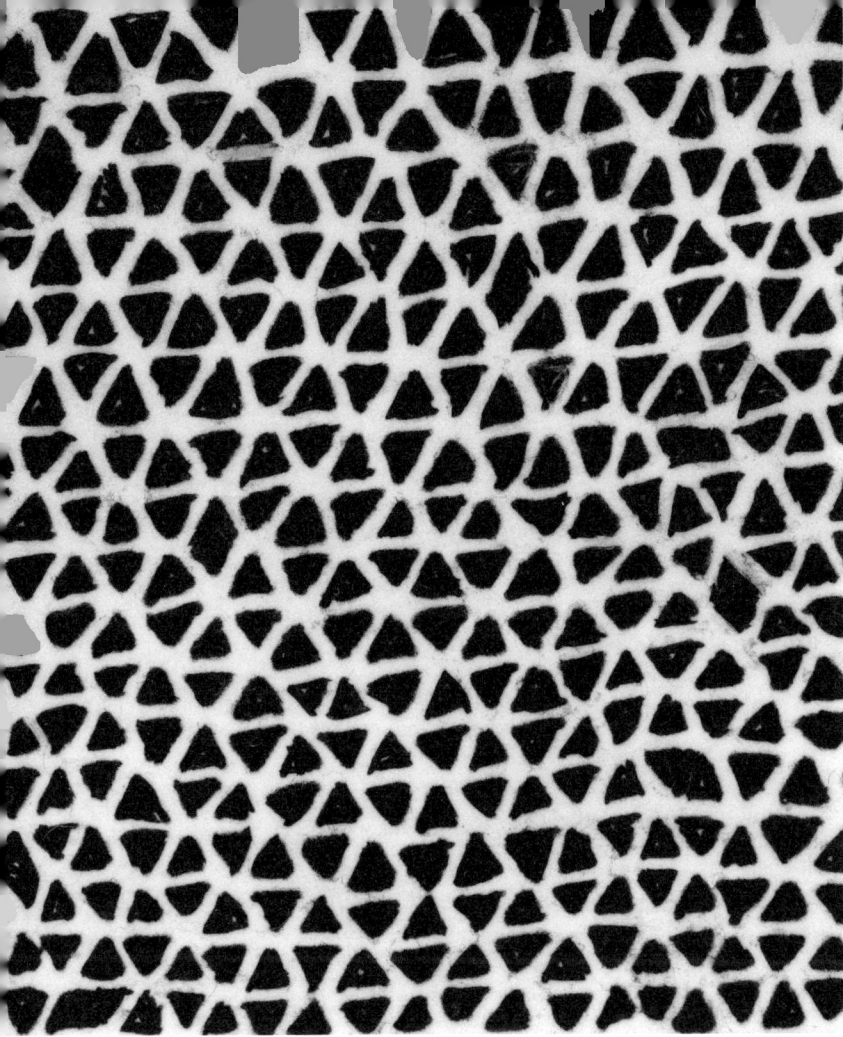

7

8

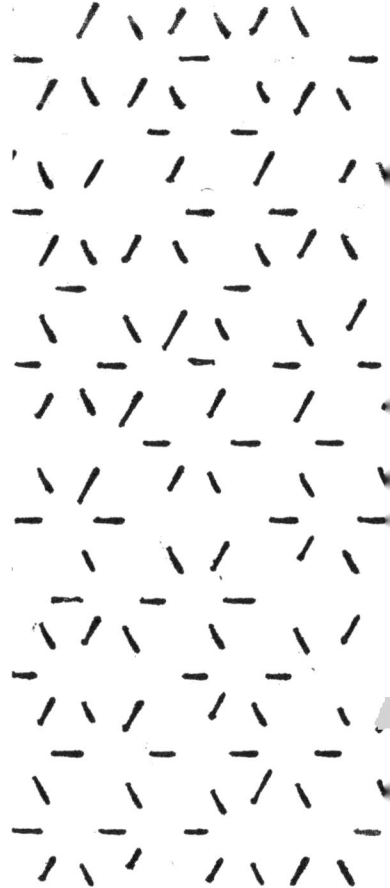

9

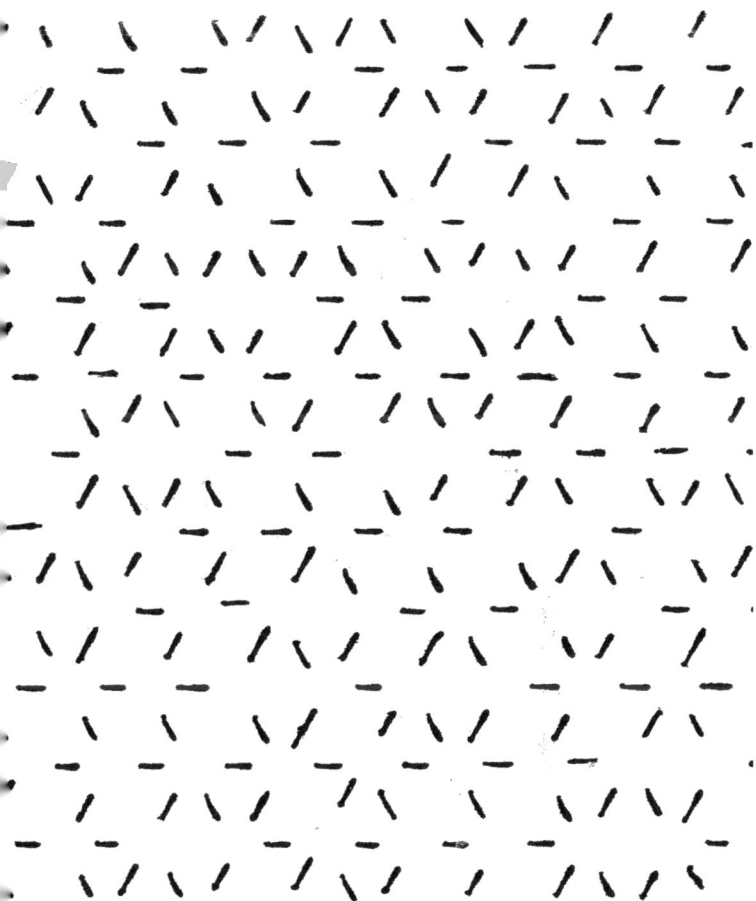

1   Triangular grid with lines
2   Triangular grid with three-pointed stars
3   Triangular grid, deformed

4   Hexagonal grid with arcs
5   Triangular grid, open
6   Triple hexagon

7   Triangular grid, free
8   Triangle from nine triangles with three points
9   Open triangular grid with short lines

1.4.3 Minimal Triangular with Planes

With a hexagon, a triangle and its doubling into a lozenge, as well as a dot matrix, a series of new options for an old subject can be found by means of division, shifting, and enlargement.

PRESENT
Computer programs can be used to precisely calculate triangular cladding of complex spatial building constructions.

PAST
In the Islamic cultural sphere, the equilateral triangle was used polychrome in all kinds of materials for floors, walls, and ceilings.

1

2

3

4

5

6

7

8

9

10

1   Large and small triangles
2   Triangular grid, free
3   Triangular grid with four triangles
4   Three-DOT grid, planar with eight to ten DOTS

5   Three-DOT grid, planar with four DOTS
6   Three-DOT grid, organic
7   Hexagonal grid, slightly shifted
8   Hexagonal grid based on a Chinese model

9   Lozenge grid, block print
10 Triangular grid, V shaped, block print

2. Geometric

GEOMETRIC, like MINIMAL, is another object-free[4] ornament group. The twelve arrangement groups already introduced in MINIMAL also apply here: FREE, STRIPED, RECTANGULAR and TRIANGULAR, with the respective subcategories WITH DOTS, WITH LINES and WITH PLANES. The statements that have already been made regarding the individual arrangement groups in MINIMAL also pertain to the GEOMETRIC groups and will not be repeated here.

Over the course of millennia, more complex geometric shapes and principles have developed from the geometrically minimalistic basis. They have achieved a new level of quality formally, yet not in principle. Today the trained eye can identify the simple geometric MINIMAL shapes everywhere in modern everyday life, whereas more complex geometric ornaments appear far less often in design, architecture and art.

When considering the history of ornaments, it becomes clear that since the Renaissance, Europe has increasingly turned away from complex, non-representational, object-free ornaments and, with recourse to Roman antiquity, has turned toward the representational floral ornament. The situation was very different in the Middle East, especially in Persia, where the complex geometric ornament was continually developed further. Inspired by my field studies, I first developed a modern geometric ornament on the basis of the square and octagon from 1974 to 2004 and, starting in 2010 with similar methodology, on the basis of the equilateral triangle.

As can be seen in the captions at the end of each chapter, the ornaments of GEOMETRIC: FREE, STRIPED and RECTANGULAR developed mainly from the square and octagon grid templates (see page 187). About two hundred classical Islamic ornaments can also be traced to these. In the GEOMETRIC: FREE, STRIPED and RECTANGULAR pilot graphics (page 159, 169 and 179), examples are presented, showing how each ornament developed from one of these grid templates. Four additional grid templates are based on the equilateral triangle. Of the four new developments, one is represented in RECTANGULAR with a sequence of triangles, squares, and pentagons (RECTANGULAR with DOTS, Figure 7), and three in TRIANGULAR, with sequences of squares and 60-degree lozenges (TRIANGULAR with DOTS, Figure 1 and TRIANGULAR with PLANES, Figure 3), of four squares and four 60-degree lozenges (TRIANGULAR with DOTS, Figure 2, and TRIANGULAR with LINES, Figure 7), and of a triangle, square, hexagon, and dodecagon (TRIANGULAR with PLANES, Figure 1, TRIANGULAR with DOTS, Figure 4, and TRIANGULAR with PLANES, Figure 7).

4   See translator's note on p. 332.

FREE with LINES

RECTANGULAR with DOTS

STRIPED with LINES

RECTANGULAR with LINES

FREE with LINES

TRIANGULAR with LINES, Regular hexagon grid

TRIANGULAR with LINES, Square and 60-degree lozenge grid

TRIANGULAR with LINES, Based on a Chinese model

TRIANGULAR with PLANES

RECTANGULAR with LINES

RECTANGULAR with LINES

RECTANGULAR with SINE WAVES

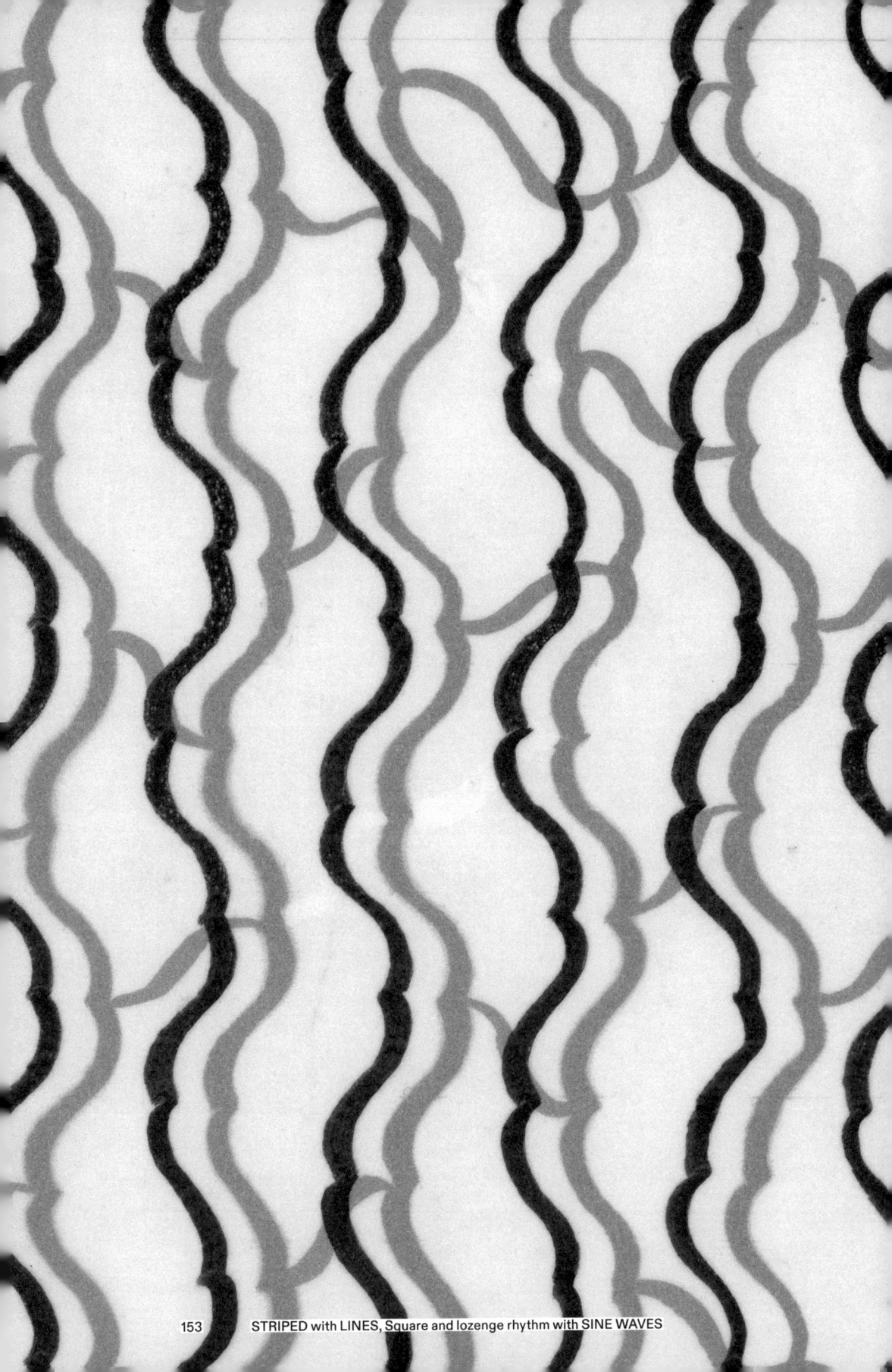

STRIPED with LINES, Square and lozenge rhythm with SINE WAVES

RECTANGULAR with DOTS, Irregular rhythm

RECTANGULAR with PLANES, Square lattice with 22.5 and 77.5 degree parallelograms

TRIANGULAR with PLANES, Three-, four-, six-, and twelve-sided sequence

TRIANGULAR with DOTS, Nine-dot square and nine-dot lozenge sequence

2. Geometric
2.1 Free

with Dots, Lines, and Planes

In GEOMETRIC: FREE, the term FREE is given a somewhat different meaning than in MINIMAL: FREE. The geometries that become more complex over time require a different kind of free arrangement from that of ornaments in MINIMAL: FREE. While in MINIMAL: FREE the recognizable ornamental arrangement appears via the similarity of the shapes used, it is impossible regarding more complex geometries to completely abandon the arrangement principle it Is based on. The result would then be a free composition and not an ornament. This means that the arrangement principle it is based on can only be freely interpreted to the degree that the ornamental arrangement remains recognizable. The arrangement principle on which most GEOMETRIC: FREE ornaments are based (page 187) is examined with the with DOTS, with LINES and with PLANES forms of presentation in a balance between free and ordered.

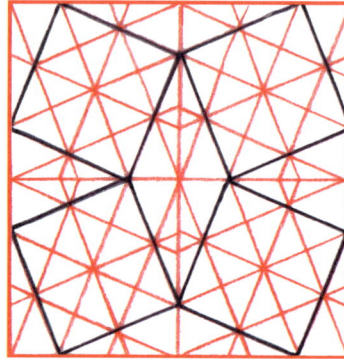

2

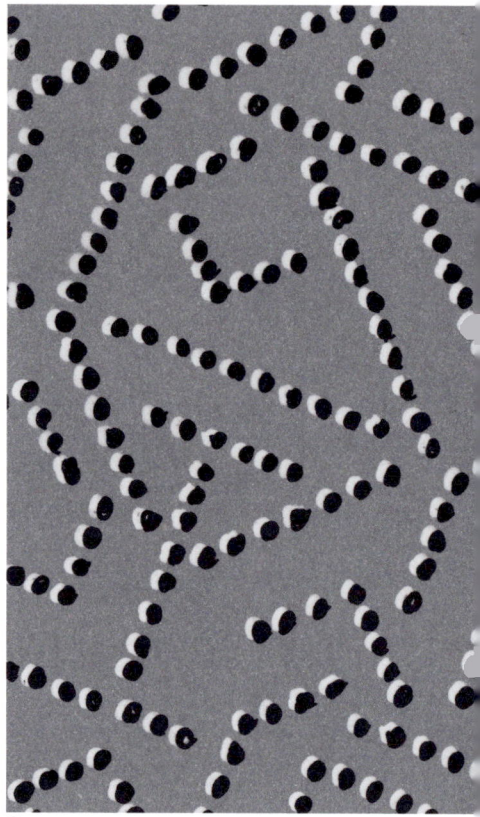

1

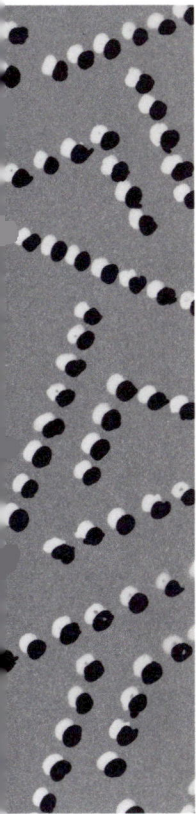

3

4

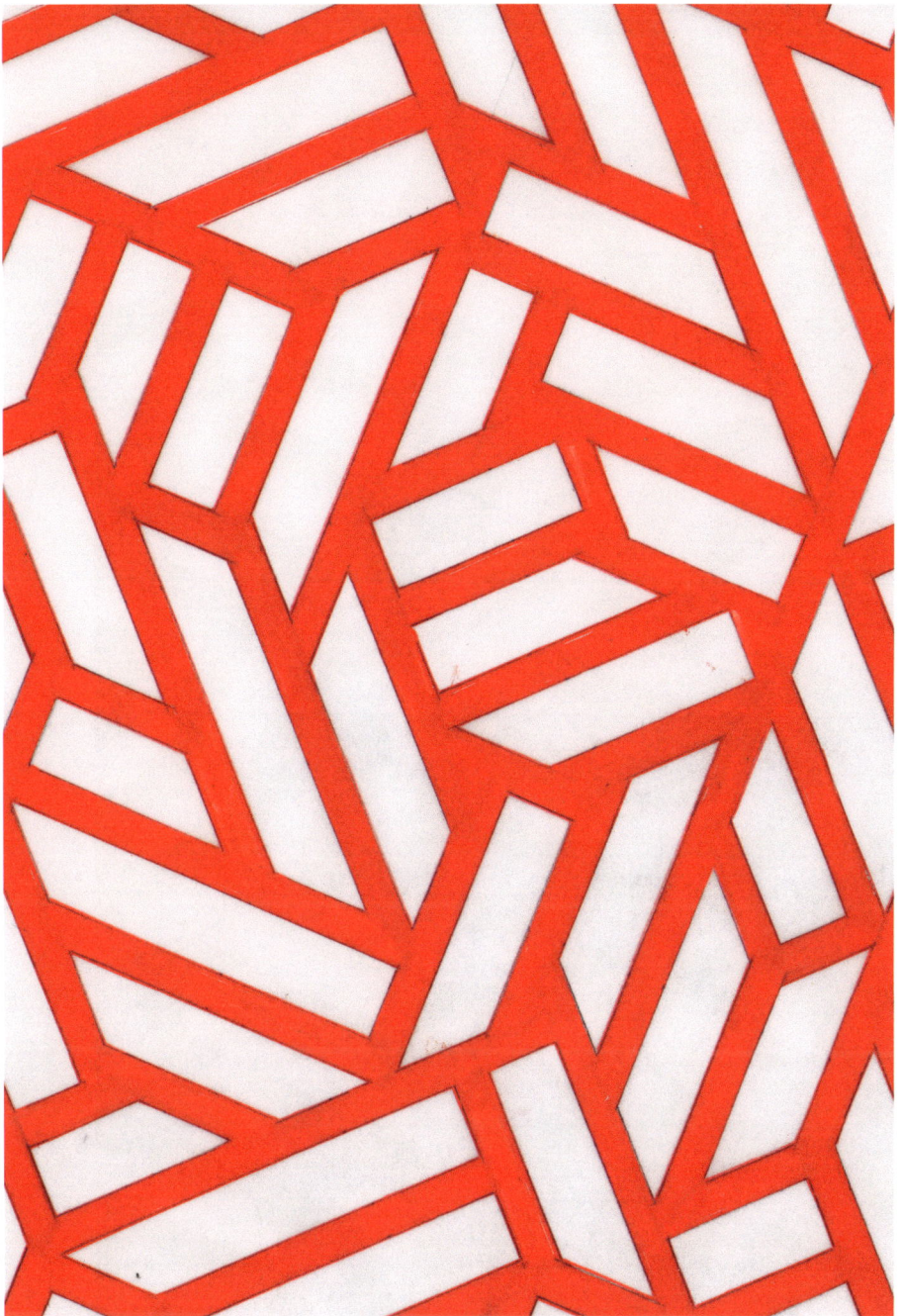

5

163   Geometric: Free

Dots, Lines, Planes

6

7

8

9

10

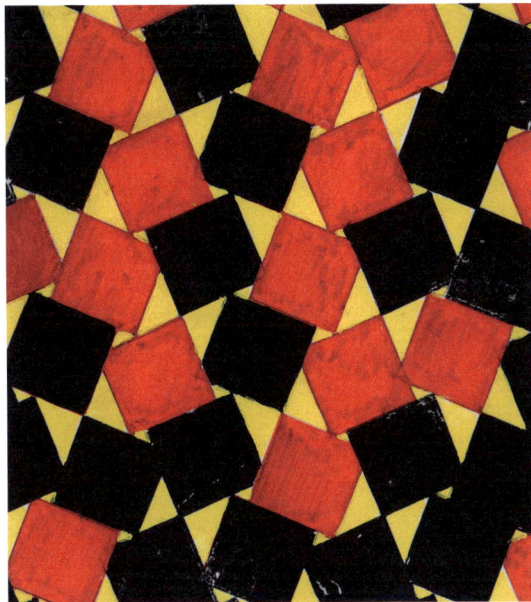

2. Geometric
2.2 Striped

with Dots, Lines, and Planes

The grid on page 187 with its square and octagonal components is interpreted as based on stripes. The results are then further elaborated into an ornamental form from the perspective of DOTS, LINES and PLANES.

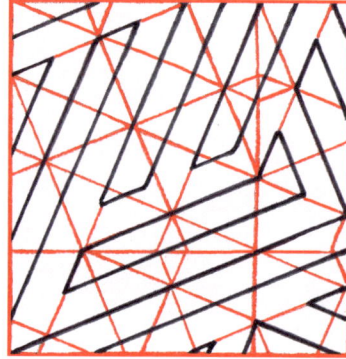

2

1

4

5

6

8

9

10

11

2. Geometric
2.3 Rectangular

The square grid on page 187 with a superimposed octagonal grid forms the basis of almost all ornaments depicted in this chapter. The interlacing of many similar Islamic octagonal ornaments led to the discovery of this basic grid, which, on the one hand, is rooted in the archaic square grid and, on the other hand, is overlaid with a more complex level of development.

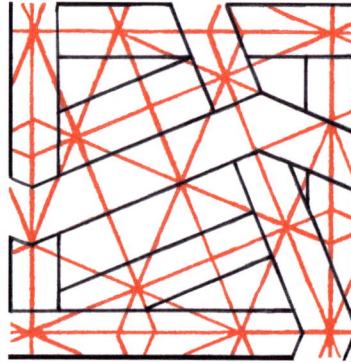

2.3.1 Geometric Rectangular with Dots

Nine illustrations show constructions based on the grid on page 187. Figure 6 shows DOTS in the shape of a cross and Figure 7 shows a triangle, square, and pentagon construction inserted into the square grid. It is known that Islamic pentagon ornaments worked with imprecision because the angles of the pentagon in the plane match neither each other nor the other shapes in 360 degrees.

2

1

3

4

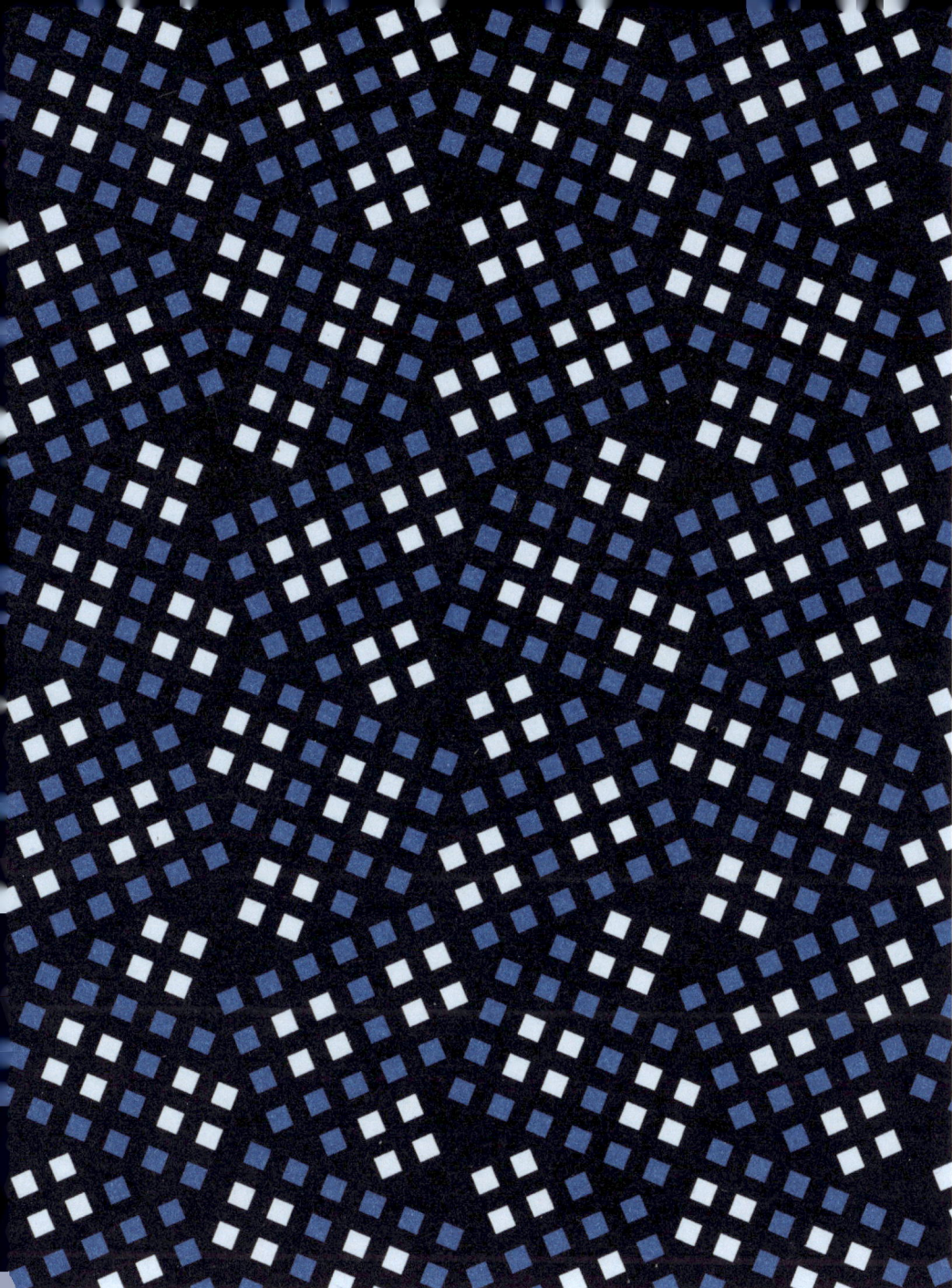

5

6

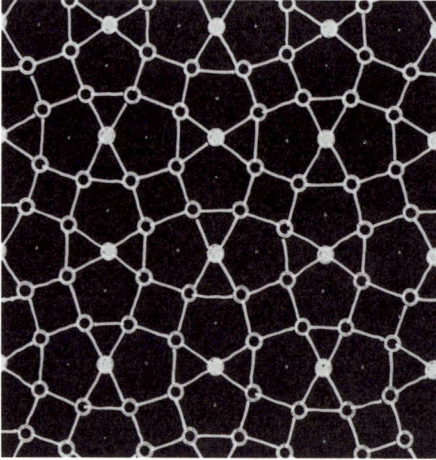

7

8

9

2.3.2 Geometric Rectangular with Lines

Seven of the eight examples were developed from the square and octagonal grid on page 187. Here the grid that forms the basis for GEOMETRIC: FREE, STRIPED and REC-TANGULAR is shown in full size.

1

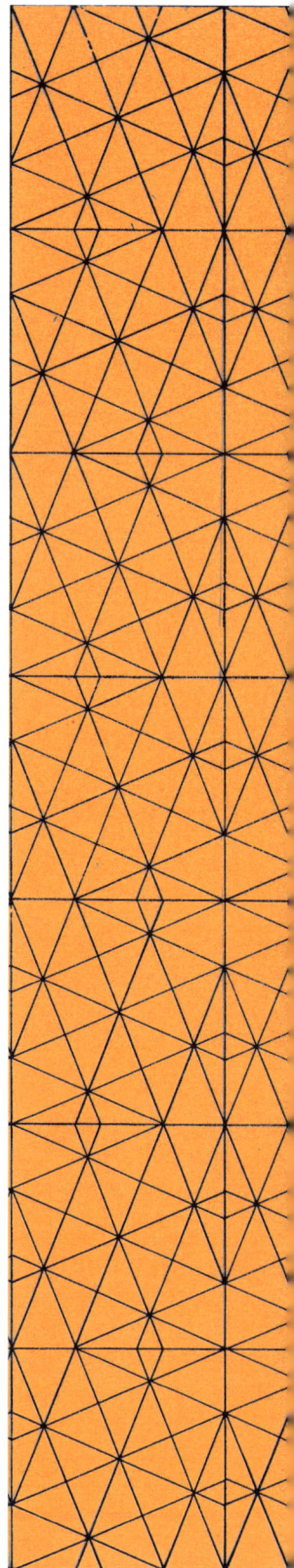

2

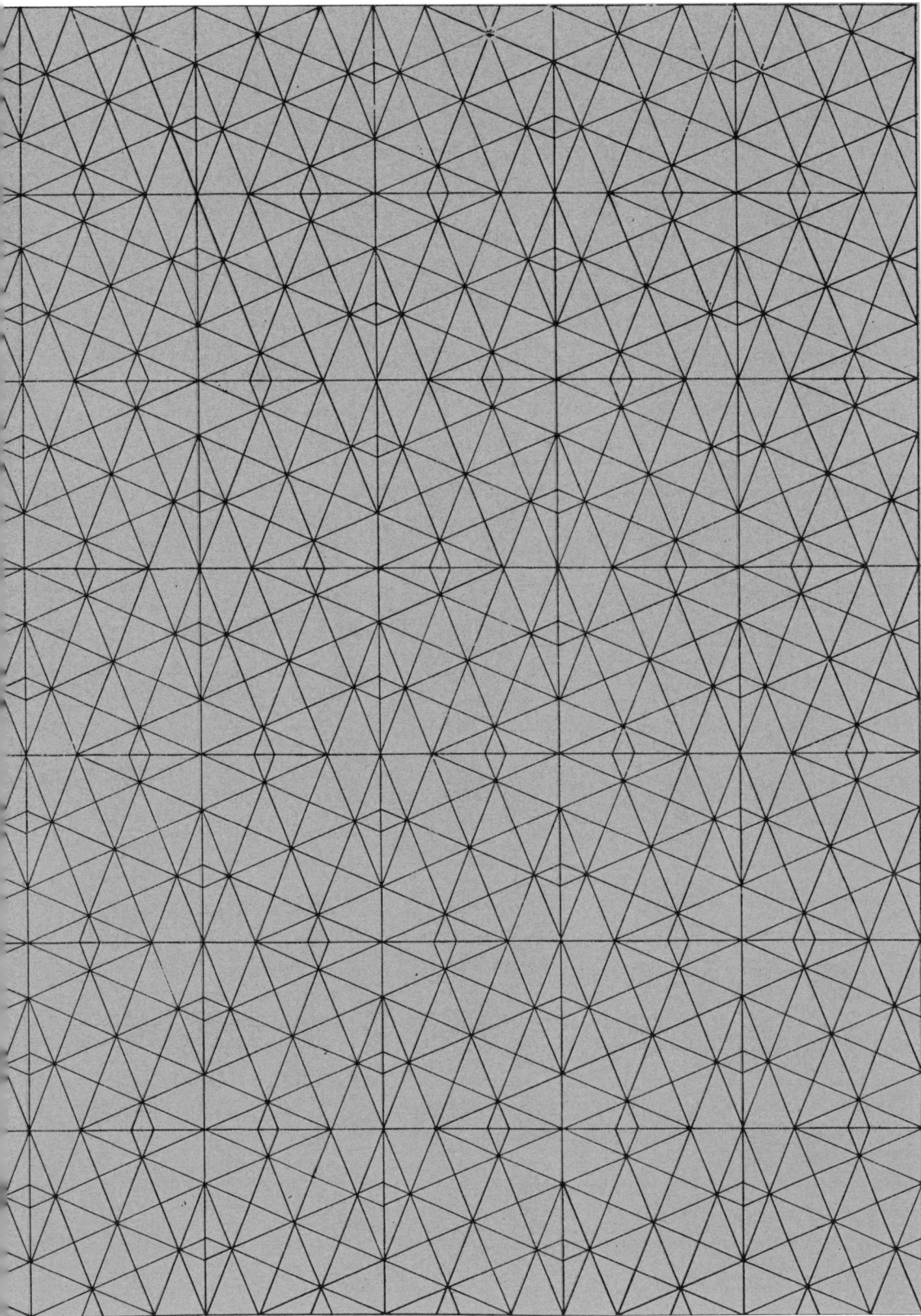

3

4

5

6

8

Lines

2.3.3 Geometric Rectangular with Planes

Six of the eight examples shown here were developed on the grid on page 187 and two were developed on graph paper.

2

1

3

4

5

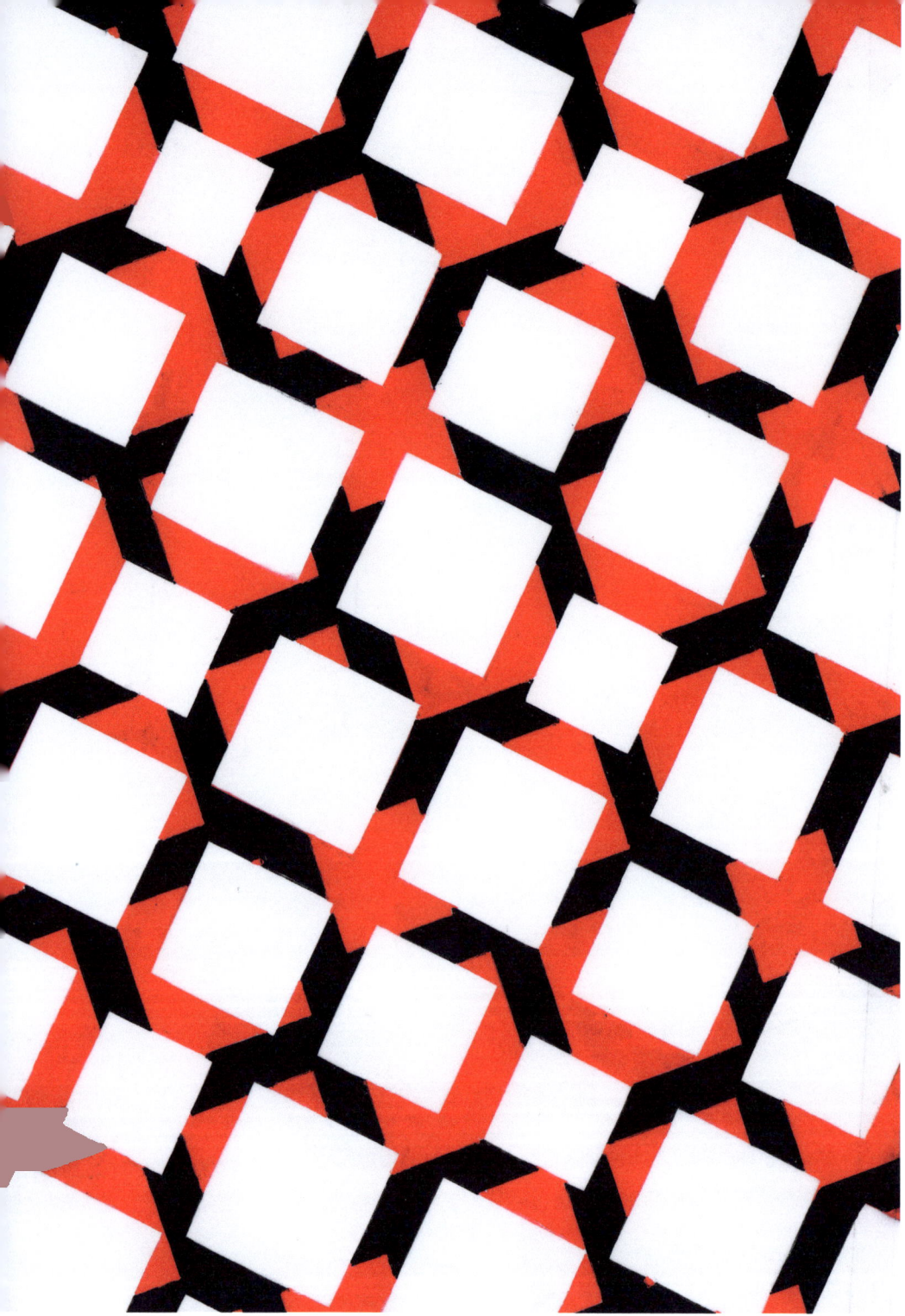

6

7

8

2.   Geometric
2.4   Triangular

GEOMETRIC: TRIANGULAR was developed on the basis of equilateral triangles or hexagons. Twenty examples take up familiar arrangements: the triangles and hexagons are ornamentally grouped with DOTS, LINES and PLANES. Seven examples generate more complex operations by adding squares. Four different ornamental principles are shown in so-called se-quences: (1) square and lozenge; (2) four squares and four lozenges; (3) six triangles, six squares laid out in a star shape around a centrally arranged hexagon to form a dodecagon; and (4) two triangles, a square and two pentagons inscribed in a square. The geo-metric shapes are emphasized either exclusively in the shape of dots or circles at their intersections, or through strings.

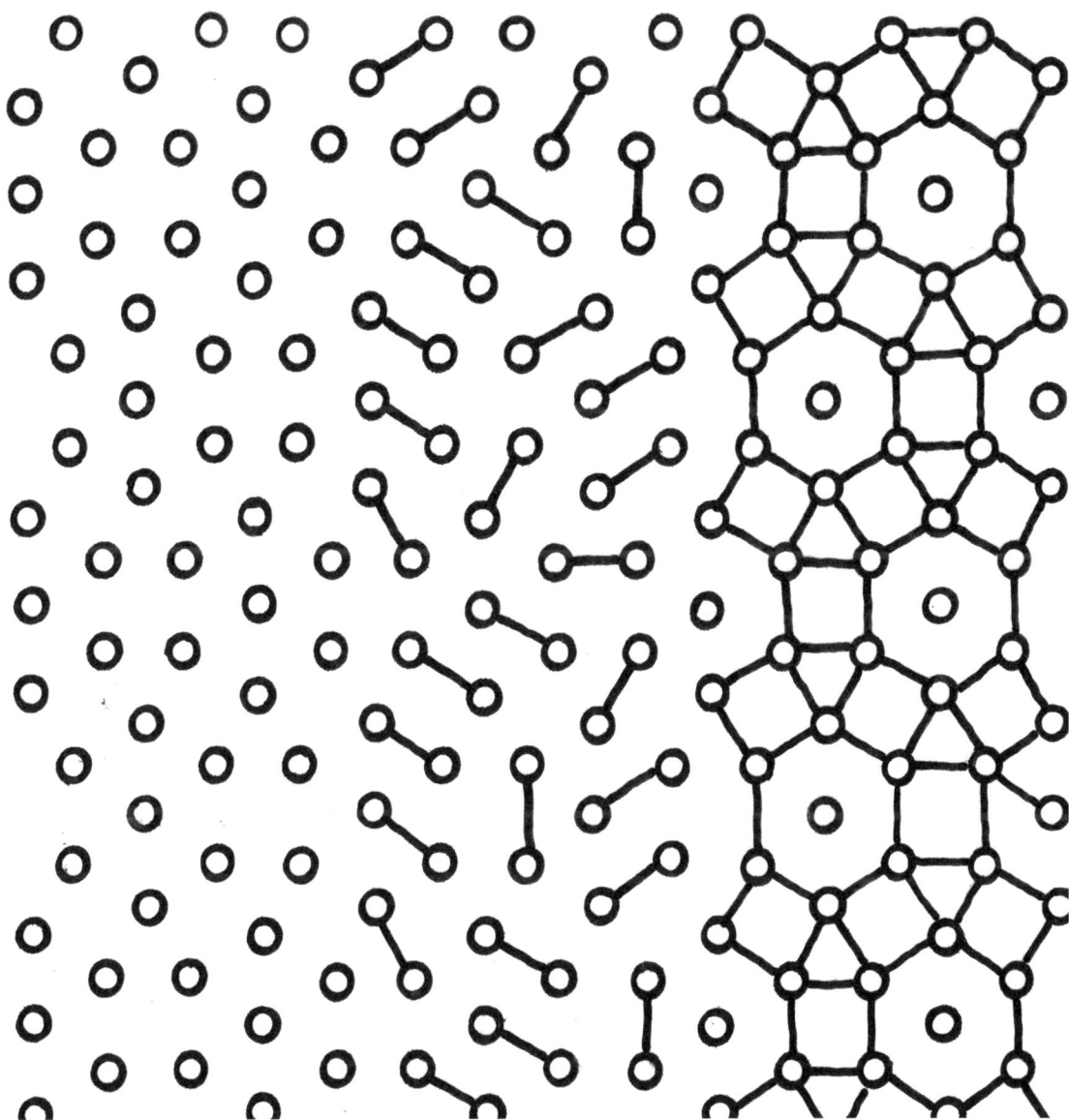

2.4.1 Geometric Triangular with Dots

Three complex dot grid ornaments (sequences of squares and lozenges; of triangle, square, hexagon, and dodecagon; as well as of four squares and four sixty-degree lozenges), and six conventional DOTS. The last-named group shows a playful way of dealing with the underlying dot grid. One of them (Figure 7) is comprised of dot formations with symbolic meaning: three dots pointing upward (male), pointing downward (female), four dots in the shape of a lozenge (thunderbolt) and five dots (hourglass).

1

3

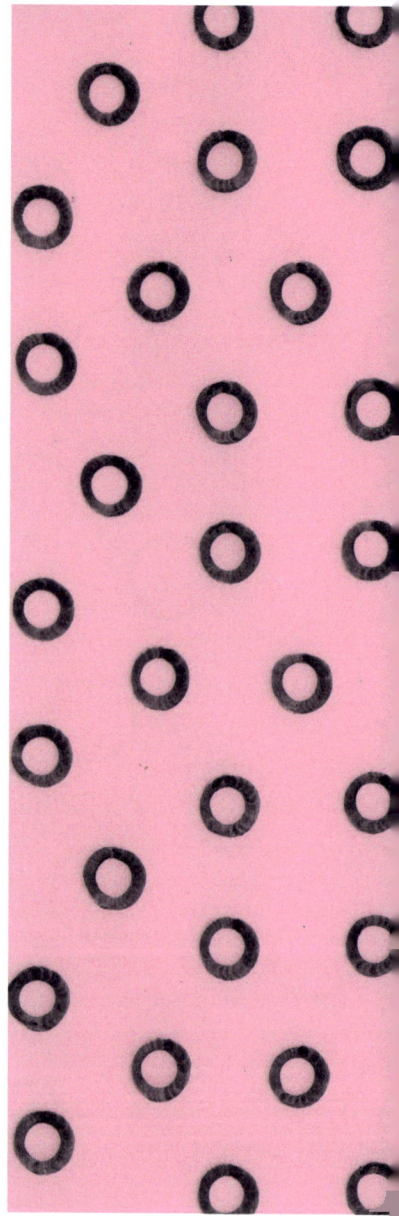

4

6

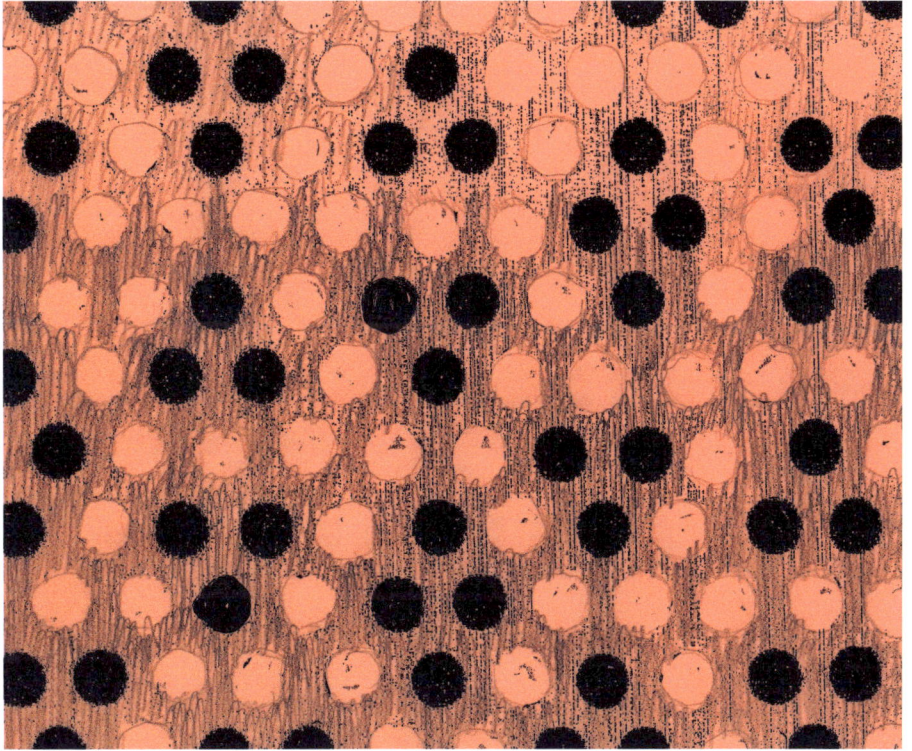

7

8

9

Dots

1   Sequence with a square and 60-degree
      lozenge in DOTS
2   Sequence with four squares and four
      60-degree lozenge in DOTS
3   Triangular grid broken down into three
      bars and three DOTS
4   Triangle, square, hexagon and dodecagon
      sequence in circles
5   Hexagon, freely interpreted
6   Hexagon, freely interpreted

7   Triangular grid focusing on symbols: male triangle,
      female triangle, hourglass and lozenge (thunderbolt)
8   Triangular grid, freely interpreted
9   On a triangular grid, DOTS connected in
      groups of four

2.4.2 Geometric Triangular with Lines

The GEOMETRIC: TRIANGULAR with LINES group consists of six conventional triangular constructions, two grids, and a complex dot matrix construction with connecting lines. Three figures from the first group are based on Chinese and Islamic ornaments, which were only slightly modified. The closed order of historical ornaments tends to be more open today.

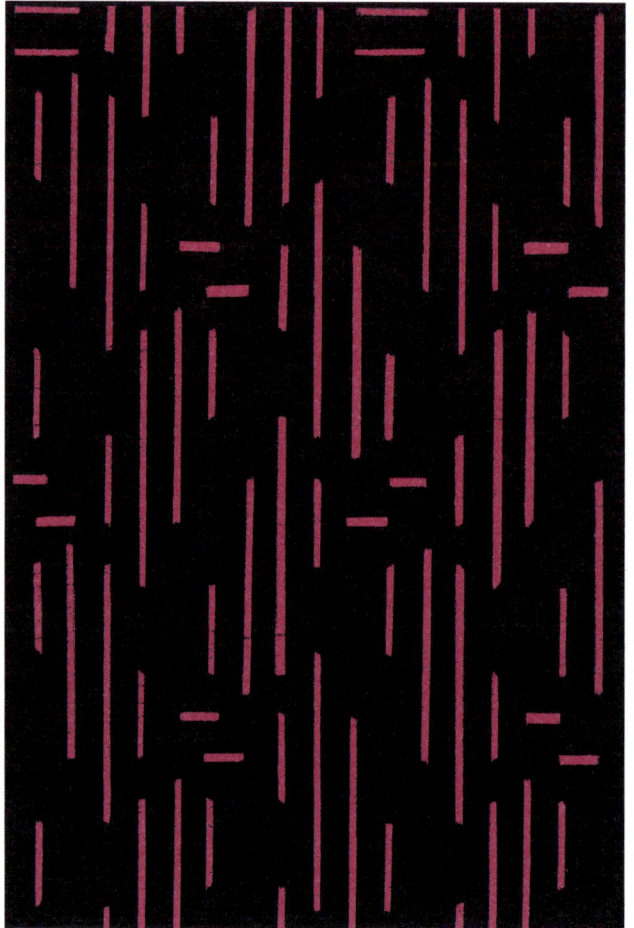

1

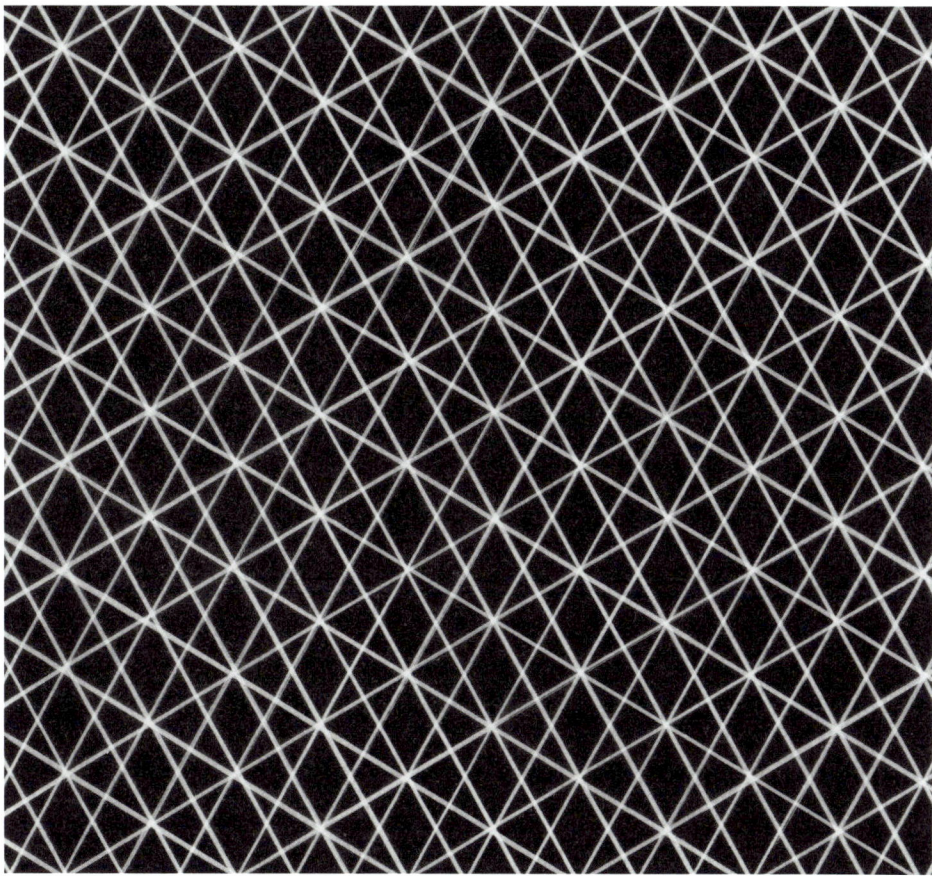

2

3

4

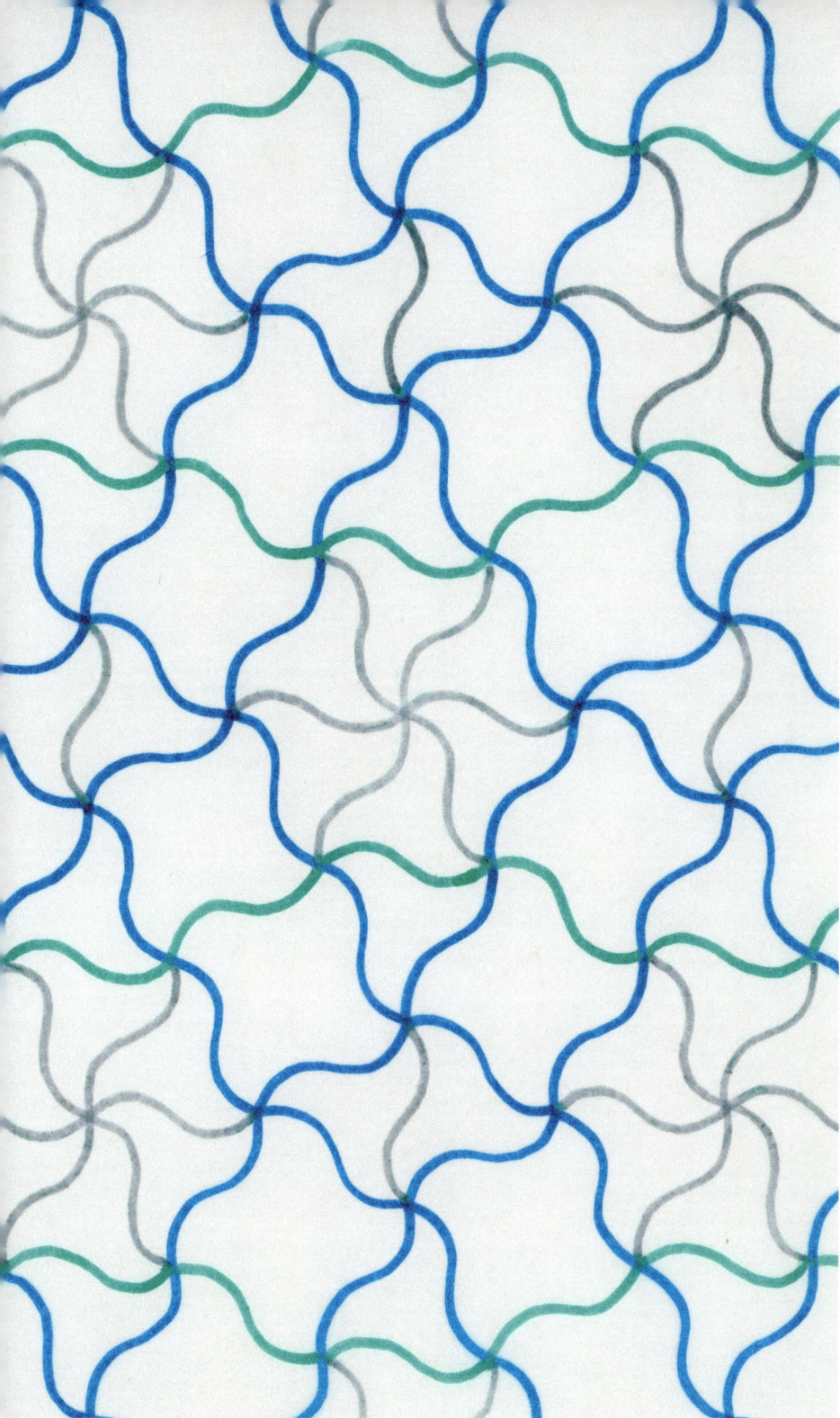

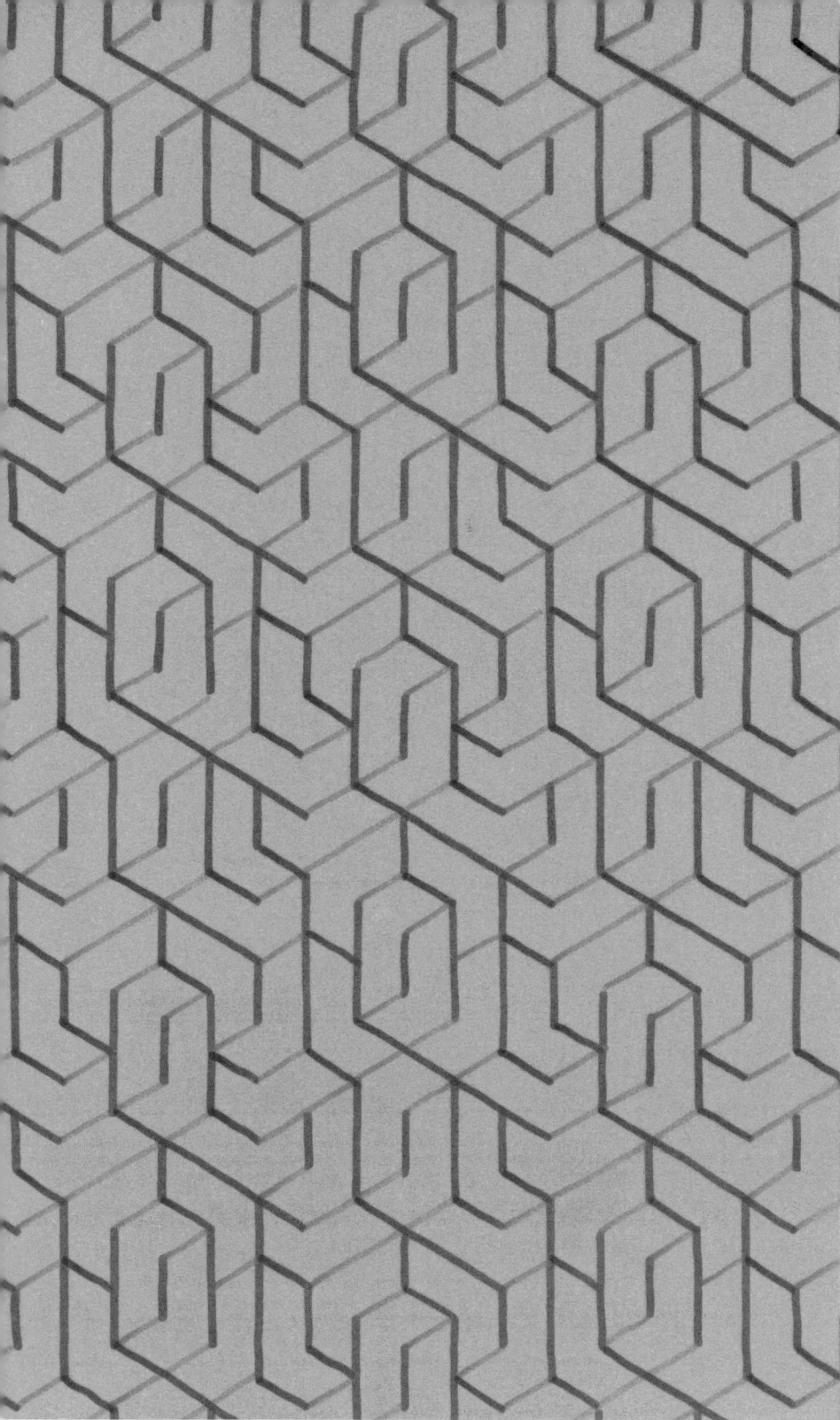

6

7

9

2.4.3 Geometric Triangular with Planes

This group is comprised of six conventional and three complex triangular ornaments. The last two examples in the first group are again based on Chinese and Islamic models (see TRIANGULAR with LINES, page 210). Of the three complex ornaments, two come from the triangle, square, hexagon, and dodecagon sequence and one is from the square and lozenge sequence.

2

1

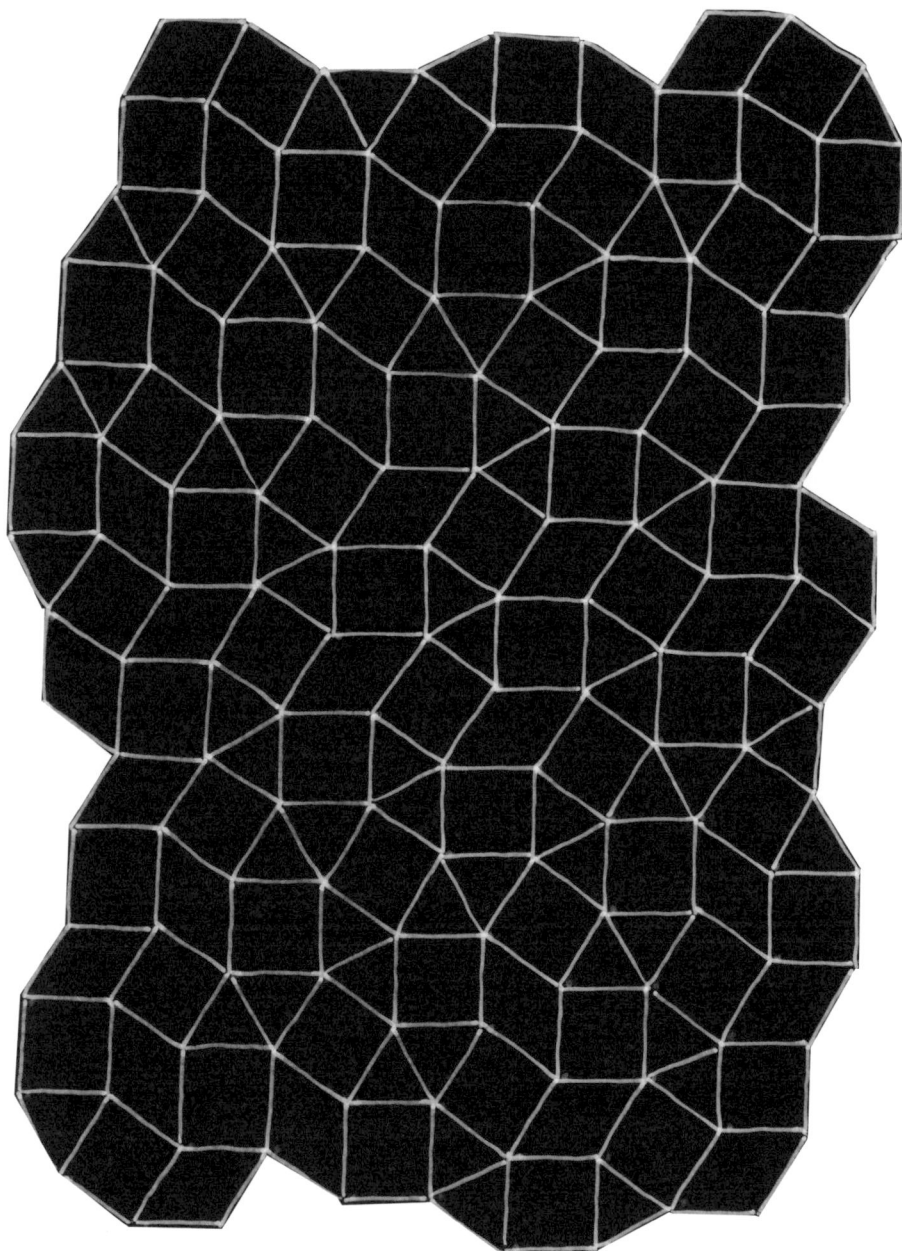

3

5

6

7

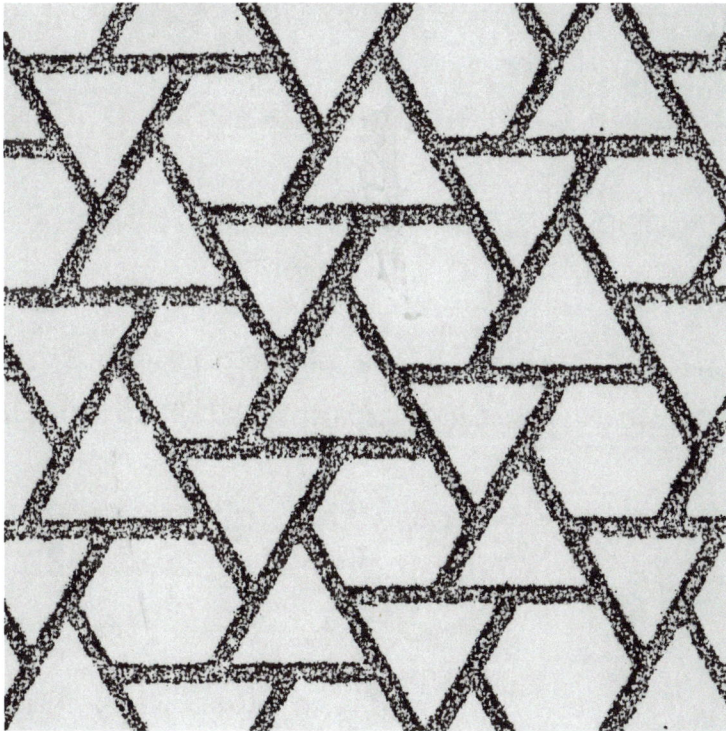

8

9

3. Floral

The central idea of *New Grammar of Ornament*, as presented in the first two chapters MINIMAL and GEOMETRIC, can also be applied to the FLORAL theme. At first glance this might not seem plausible, as it concerns a completely different visual world. The fitting division of MINIMAL and GEOMETRIC into FREE, STRIPED, RECTANGULAR and TRIANGULAR always resonates in the background, as does the breakdown into DOTS, LINES and PLANES. And yet this does not allow the construction of an adequate grammar for FLORAL. Here, appropriate categories need to be developed and distinctive related groups and shapes identified. In doing this, several focuses emerge from the diversity of floral shapes: flowers, now called SUNS, from the front and the side, PLANTS with leaves and vines, ARCHETYPES and the quaternity of the planet EARTH: water, air, earth and fire. Ornaments that connect flora with animals and human beings were not included in the canon.

Whereas regarding object-free[5] ornaments, a square from prehistoric times is still a square today, floral ornamental shapes underwent a shift over the course of millennia. *The New Grammar of Ornament* nevertheless does not want to offer an evolutionary history, but instead provide a contemporary contribution: What significance do the old forms still have today? For example, let us look at the most well-known motif, a flower in full bloom viewed from the front. Its circular shape developed thousands of years ago from a symbol for the sun, and it continues to mirror tranquility, perfection and greatness.

From the great abundance of floral ornaments, a manageable cosmos will be compiled in four chapters. It is based on the insight into the difference between that which is constructive on the basis of clear laws, and the floral diversity that is decisive for the floral ornament. This includes, on the one hand, geometric laws without any visible resemblance to the diversity of creation and, on the other hand, the abundance of shapes that initially resist any constructive notions. This makes it necessary to accept the diversity and acknowledge traditional groups such as flowers, leaves, vines and fruits as laws. Also, however, the ornamental floral world must be recognized as a constructive set of building blocks of individual shapes, a set that allows every type of floral combination, whether flowers and fruits, leaves and fruits, or just fruits. In that, it is important to consider the successful design of an individual shape, such as that of a leaf, as seriously as the combinability with other individual shapes. The discovery of this global set of building blocks, which every culture, every epoch and every social stratum has made use of and continues to be able to use, and with which every combination is possible in principle,

is the contribution of this *New Grammar of Ornament* to the floral ornament.

Floral ornaments most often use a free arrangement. The idea of a "repeating pattern" used to be important, since weaving and printing ornaments on fabric and wallpaper only functioned with manageably sized print models, screens or rollers. The repeating patterns used were linear, rectangular or triangular. The question of repeating patterns has today lost significance through the use of computer programs.

Some floral elements can be correctly identified botanically, and at times epochs such as the gothic (1200–1500 CE) attached great importance to a closeness to nature. In general, however, these were mere exceptions. With respect to style-setting examples from Persian and Chinese traditions regarding textiles, rugs and ceramics, then nothing here fits together botanically. No flower or leaf matches its neighbor. Moreover, flowers and leaves outdo each other with their fantasy shapes and forms, and on top of that they are aligned on thin vines that in reality could not support a single one of the lush flowers or leaves. All of this fits well with the characteristic feature of floral ornaments: the surreal.

The floral building blocks allow for both simple and elaborate designs. A design is considered simple if only shapes from one group are combined, and it is elaborate if different groups all play a role. In the following, the more simple combinations are treated in the individual chapters, and the more elaborate combination in the preceding eighteen pages of poetics.

5 See translator's note on p. 332

SUNS with THREE LOBES and FOUR LOBES

MISCELLANEOUS, Turkish model

SPIRALS and MISCELLANEOUS

231   SUNS with FOUR LOBES and SINE WAVES

SUNS with THREE LOBES and FOUR LOBES

FRUITS and LEAVES

SUNS with THREE LOBES, LEAVES and SPIRALS

SUNS with THREE LOBES and MISCELLANEOUS

LEAVES and OVALS

FRUITS and LEAVES

SUNS with THREE LOBES, FOUR LOBES and FRUITS

SUNS with EIGHT LOBES, SUNS with THREE LOBES, FLOWERS and LEAVES

SUNS with FIVE LOBES and SINE WAVES

3.   Floral
3.1   Suns

In order to do justice to the diversity, a series of botanically familiar flower shapes have been compiled: the octagon, hexagon, pentagon, square and the triangle with a simple outline and an abstract interior.

PRESENT
The aforementioned aspect of mirroring (see page 227) is best reflected in the round blossom. This is why it assumes a key position in design. Should it take on a more lush, elaborate form such as that of a chrysanthemum? Or a reduced, less botanical form? Which variant fits into today's new set of building blocks?

PAST
The European floral tradition traces back largely to Italian fabrics, which in turn had their models since the High Middle Ages in Syria and Egypt. The Near East has long enjoyed a Persian-Chinese influence. The first sun signs came from Mesopotamia and Anatolia.

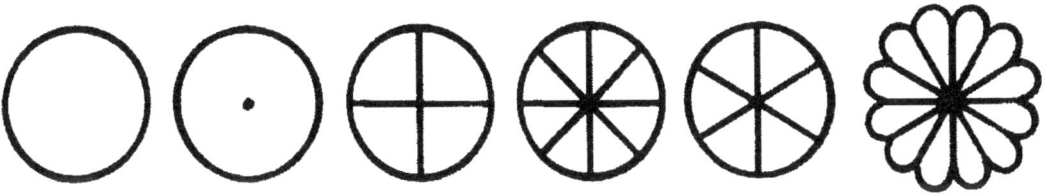

247   Floral: Suns

3. Floral
3.1 Suns

3.1.1   with Eight Lobes

The largest flower viewed from the front is shown in sixteen variations.

PRESENT
FLORAL: SUNS with EIGHT LOBES principle appears in the flower of clematis and the fruit of star anise.

PAST
The oldest circle with eight rays came from Mesopotamia and was the graphic sign for God (2500 BCE). In Islamic art, the sun in geometric shapes was very widespread (See page 247).

3.1.1   with Eight Lobes
        Cloth, stamped with resistant
        material such as wax, Ivory Coast

1

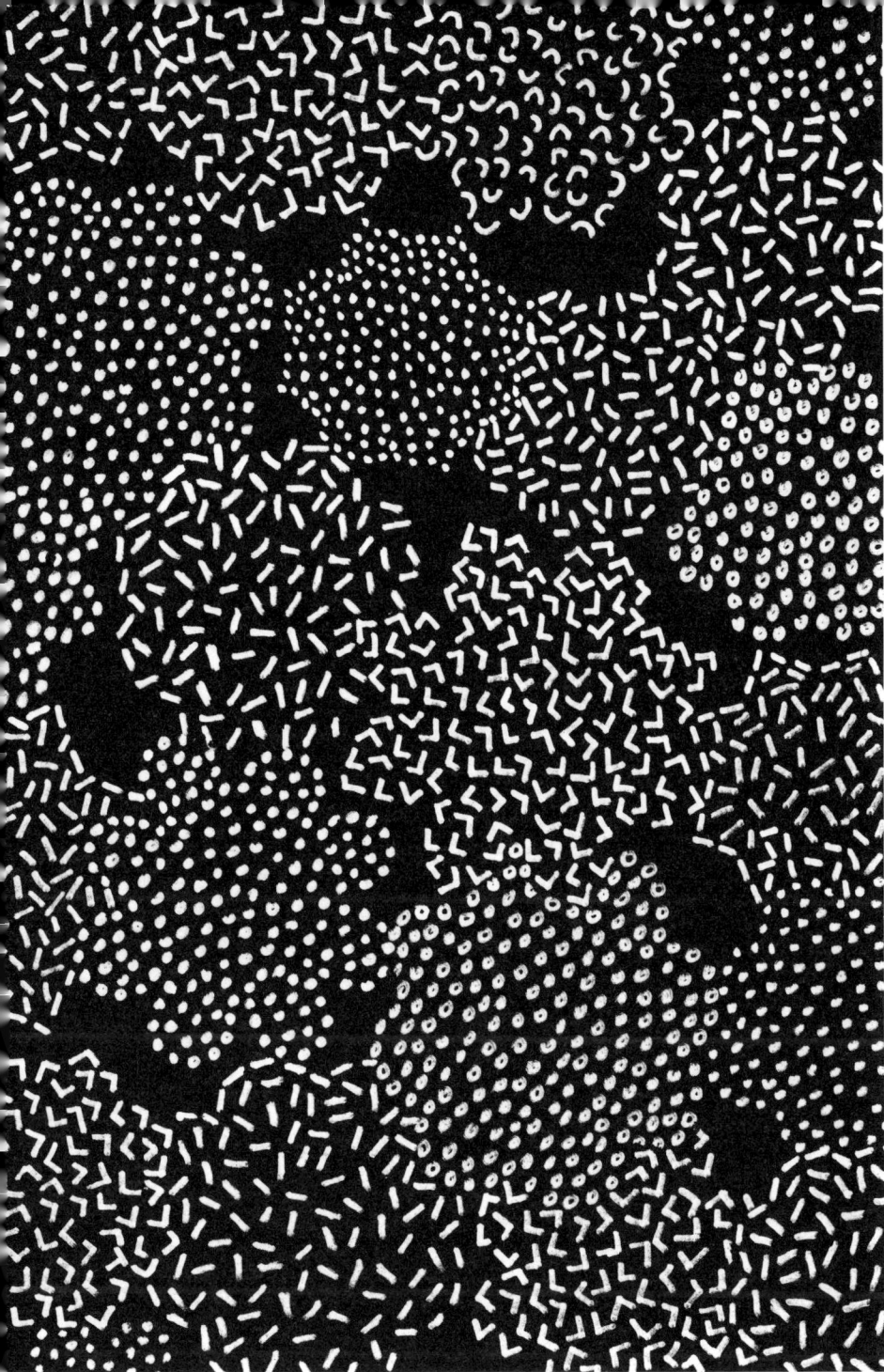

2

3

4

1   SUNS with EIGHT LOBES, filled with lines
2   SUNS with EIGHT LOBES, SUNS in DOTS and LINES

3   SUNS with EIGHT LOBES, transparent
4   SUNS with EIGHT LOBES, linear

3. Floral
3.1 Suns

3.1.2 with Six Lobes

Flowers with six petals are represented here in an abstract form, also in MINIMAL: TRIANGULAR and GEOMETRIC: TRIANGULAR. As a FLORAL: SUN it is shown in eighteen varieties.

PRESENT
The flower with six petals is the most popular in design and also the most widespread botanical shape, also with respect to cut flowers such as tulips and lilies.

PAST
Due to its strict symmetrical shape and simple repeating pattern, the FLORAL: SUNS with SIX LOBES arrangement is popular especially in folk art ornaments.

3.1.2   with Six Lobes
Ceramic mosaic in mosque, Konya,
Turkey, 15th century

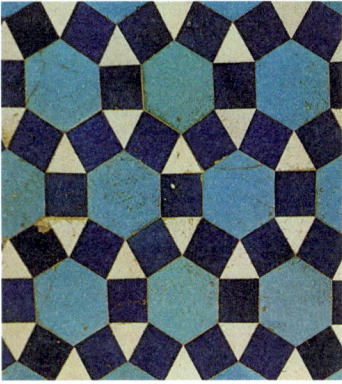

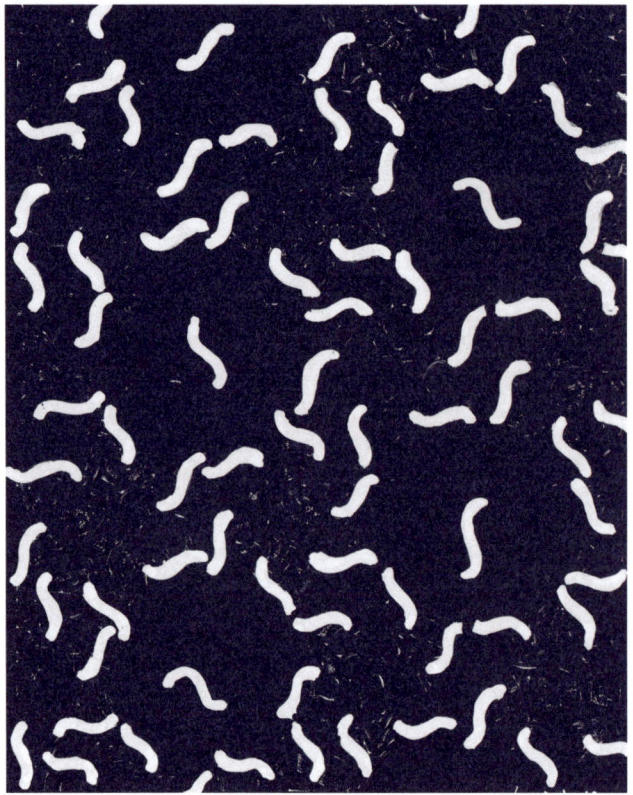

1

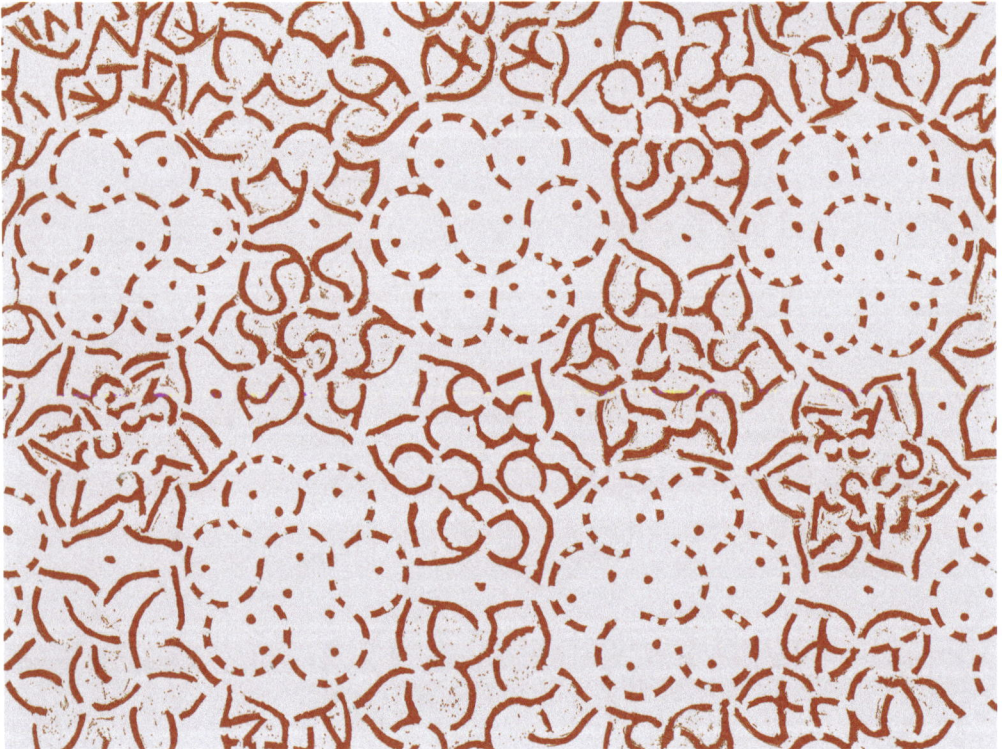

2

3

6 Lobes

1   SUNS with SIX LOBES linear in SINE WAVES
2   SUNS with SIX LOBES in LINES and DOTS
3   SUNS with SIX LOBES linear on a 60-degree
     lozenge grid

3. Floral
3.1 Suns

The asymmetrical shape of FLORAL: SUNS with FIVE LOBES is inspiring for open arrangements. Here it is shown in twenty-five varieties.

PRESENT
Almost all edible fruits develop from a flower with five petals. The artist Andy Warhol made the shape popular. In the shape of a star it also decorates the flag of the United States.

PAST
This shape has been known through its use as defensive magic (pentagram) and 3-dimensionally as one of the five Platonic solids (dodecahedron) since the New Stone Age.

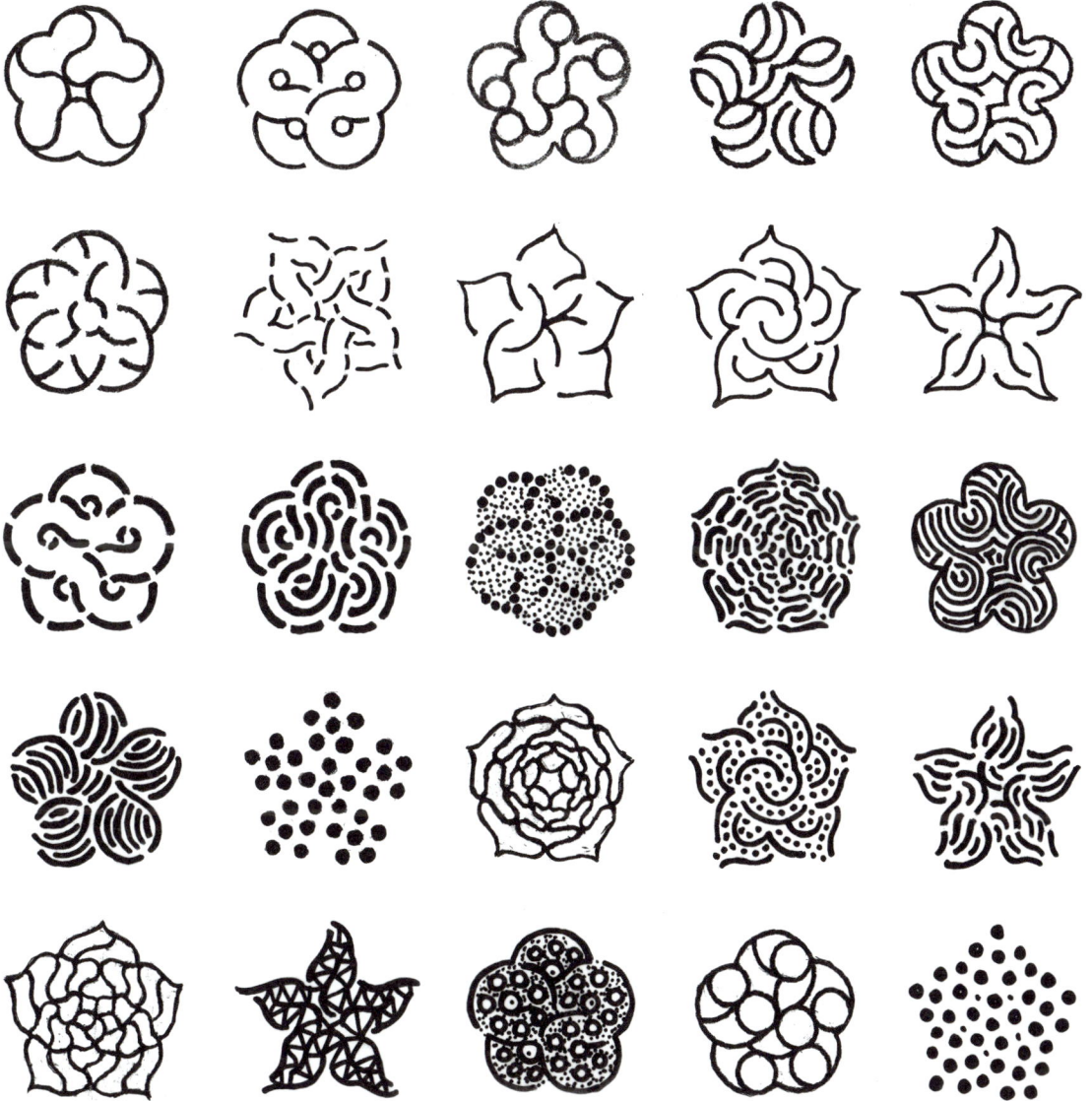

1

2

3

4

5

1 SUNS with FIVE LOBES in LINES and DOTS
2 SUNS with FIVE LOBES in PLANES

3 SUNS with FIVE LOBES in composition
4 SUNS with FIVE LOBES in composition

5 SUNS with FIVE LOBES in TRIANGULAR DOT grid

3. Floral
3.1 Suns

3.1.4   with Four Lobes

FLORAL: SUNS with FOUR LOBES offer many options through its proximity to a square and the shape
of a cross. Twenty-seven varieties are shown here.

PRESENT
The artist Henri Matisse popularized the FLORAL:
SUNS with FOUR LOBES principle. As a flower it exists in the crucifers, for example, cabbage. It is the
classical ornamental tile shape.

PAST
In medieval glass and book paintings, this principle
was popular as a repeating pattern and as a quatrefoil
in tracery windows.

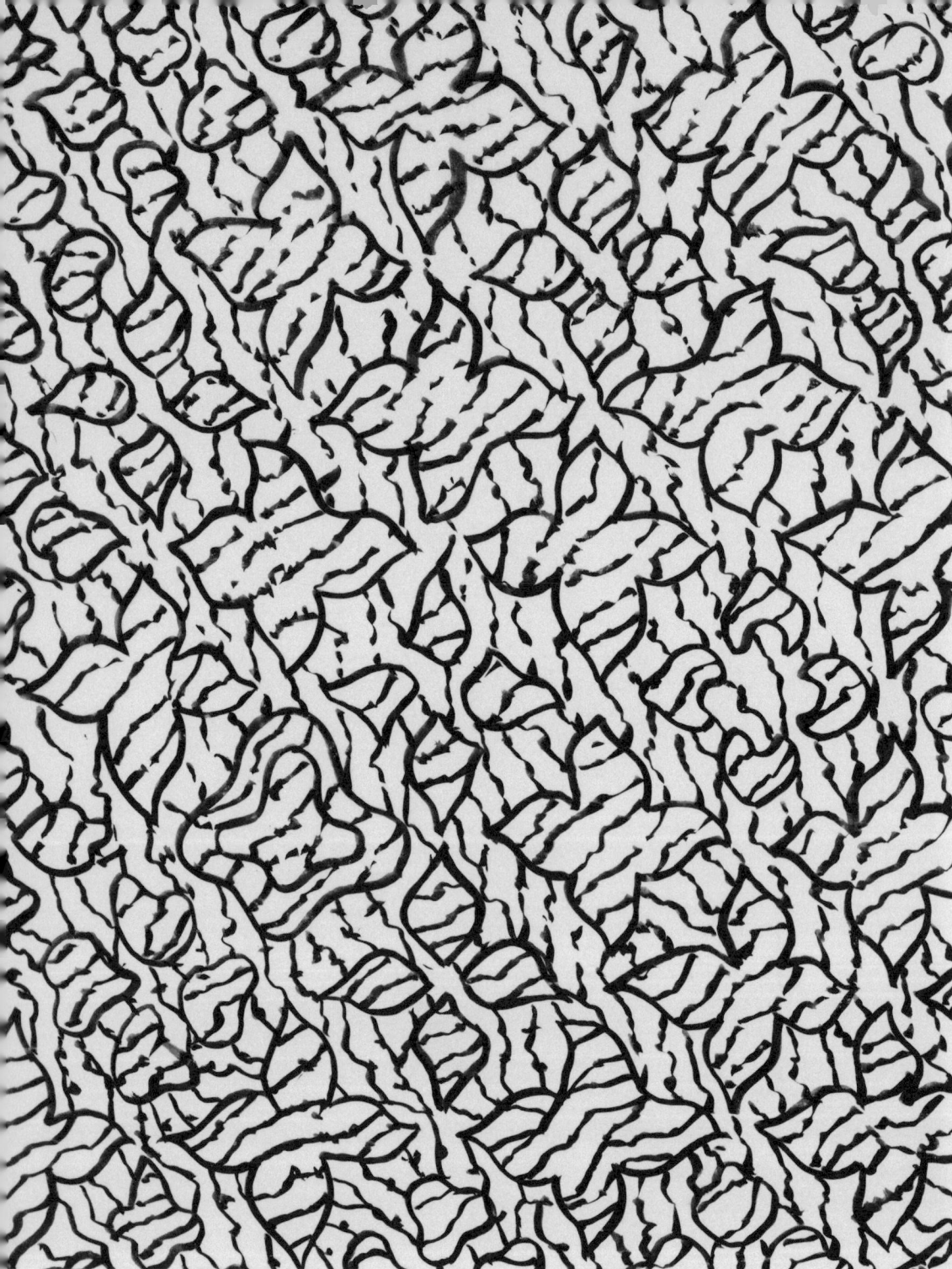

1

4 Lobes

3   SUNS with FOUR LOBES, linear and DOTS

1   SUNS with FOUR LOBES, filled with LINES
2   SUNS with FOUR LOBES, linear

3. Floral
3.1 Suns

This principle is shown in twenty-five variations.

PRESENT
FLORAL: SUNS with THREE LOBES are popular as an endless ornamental pattern in the Far East. The most famous example of this trefoil shape is the Mercedes star from Daimler Benz, followed by the symbols for radioactivity and for blindness.

PAST
In the Middle Ages, the FLORAL: SUNS with THREE LOBES were popular in stained glass and window shapes as a symbol of the Trinity.

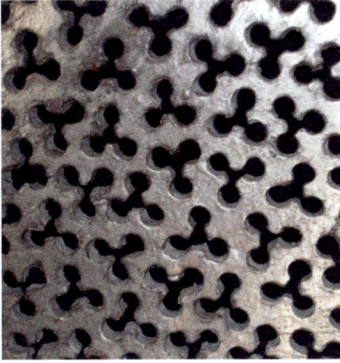

 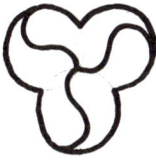   

2

1

3

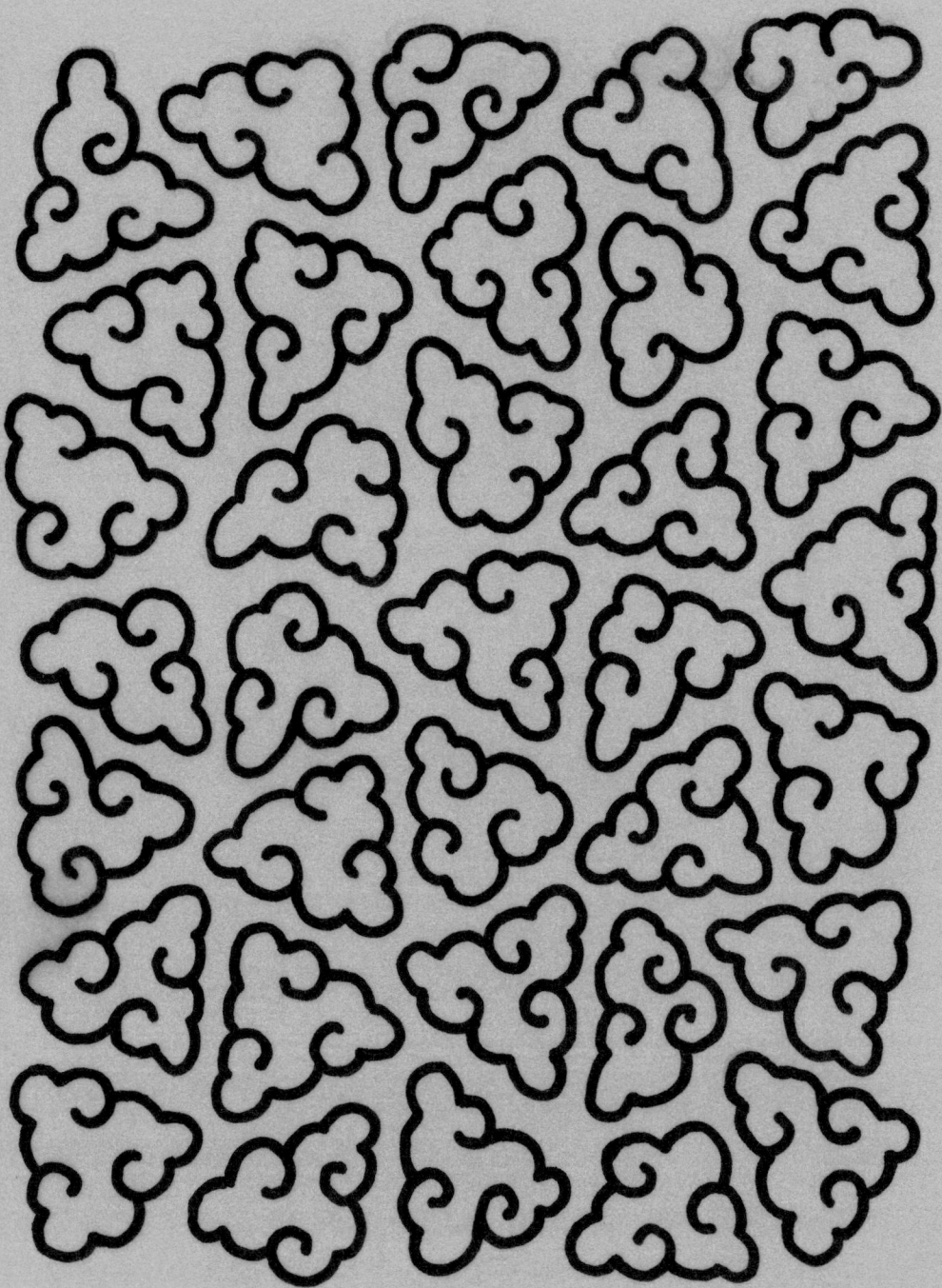

4

5

3 Lobes

6

7

8

1 SUNS with THREE LOBES in LINES consisting of two forms in three parts

2 SUNS with THREE LOBES in LINES consisting of two forms in three parts

3 SUNS with THREE LOBES in LINES

4 SUNS with THREE LOBES in spiral shape, based on a Chinese model

5 SUNS with THREE LOBES in two parts

6 SUNS with THREE LOBES, combination of 21 variations

7 SUNS with THREE LOBES in spiral shape, based on a Chinese/African model

8 SUNS with THREE LOBES, combination of 23 variations

3. Floral
3.2 Plants

3.2.1 with Flowers and Fruits
3.2.2 with Leaves and Branches

Instead of a reduction, the focus is more on greater diversity in shape and detail. Twenty-five different fruits and flowers, twenty-seven shapes of leaves and thirty-three vines offer a manageable cosmos whose shapes can easily be combined with each other.

PRESENT
Compositions of the floral ornament have changed over the last hundred years. Moving away from a main motif with large flowers surrounded by accessories such as leaves and vines, from flora consisting of flowers and plants; and moving toward flora as the world of plants. What used to be the background is now the main focus. Leaves and flowers are now usually only outlines lacking any details.

PAST
The clear-cut in floral ornamentation a century ago in the West led to a loss in shapes, colors and compositions there, which the Near and Far East did not experience. Instead of developing new designs in the West, the shelves in shops there became filled with fabrics, dishes and paper from the Far East.

3. Floral
3.2 Plants

3.2.1 with Flowers and Fruits

Looking at FRUITS and FLOWERS from the side is less engaging than the view from the front. A selection of twelve FRUITS and thirteen FLOWERS in side view thus offers a good opportunity to consider them.

PRESENT
The distinction between FLOWERS and FRUITS no longer seems to be formally significant. A large selection of shapes will nevertheless be presented here.

PAST
FRUITS and FLOWERS depicted from the side were welcome as a creative means in order to more easily integrate the large FLOWERS in front view into the surrounding foliage.

3.2.1   with Flowers and Fruits
French book with Persian and
Indian flower design, 19th century

1

2

3

4

5

Flowers and Fruits

1   FRUITS, outlined
2   FRUITS in LINES, filled

3   12 different FRUITS on LEAVES
4   FLOWERS, combination of thirteen variations

5   FLOWERS in DOTS

3. Floral
3.2 Plants

3.2.2 with Leaves and Branches

From 27 LEAF and 33 VINE variations, even the most simple compositions can be given a new look.

PRESENT
A focus on minimalism meant that the outlines and structures of leaf shapes were tremendously reduced. The Italian designer Ettore Sottsass introduced minimal ornament design in the 1980s with the Memphis Milano Group.

PAST
Chinese and Persian artists were masters in examining and abstracting from plant forms; parallel to nature they created their own, richer world of shapes.

1

2

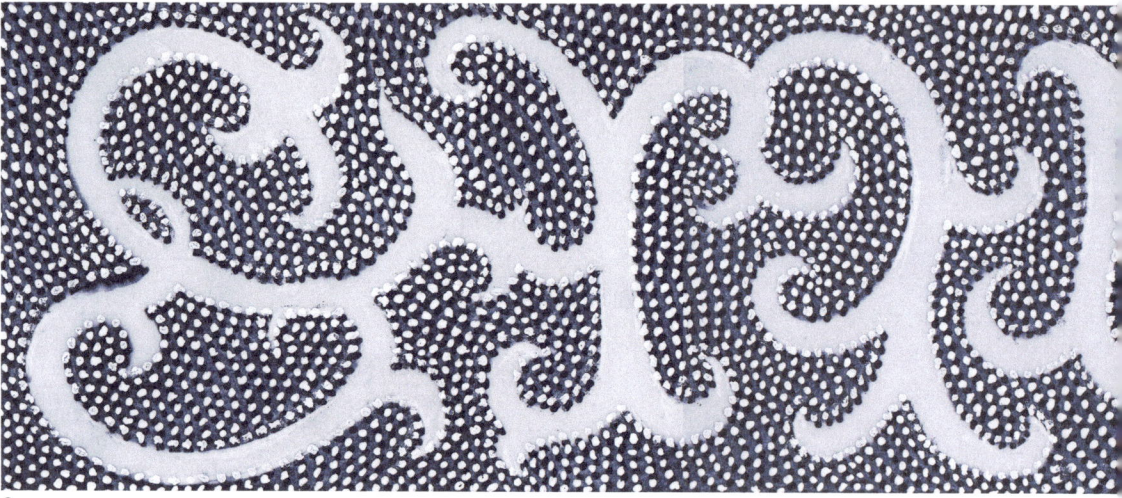

3

4

5

6

7

1   Combination with 27 variations
2   LEAVES in DOTS, based on a model of
     William Morris

3   Persian LEAVES, doubled in rows
4   Persian LEAVES, taken as PLANTS
5   BRANCHES, based on a medieval European model

6   Persian LEAVES and BRANCHES
7   BRANCHES, skeleton of Figure 5

3. Floral
3.3 Archetypes

With 25 SINE shapes, 30 OVAL shapes, 28 SPIRAL shapes and 24 MISCELLANEOUS shapes, an established treasure of shapes gains new content, and with more than a hundred individual figures they enrich the ornamental floral canon. With a timeless shape located between MINIMAL and FLORAL, FLORAL: ARCHETYPES opens up a third group between object-free geometric ornaments and representational floral ornaments.

PRESENT
Between object-free[6] geometric ornaments and representational floral ornaments there is yet another group of old, abstract and strongly symbolic signs. They are not directly floral, but their organic forms make them part of the wider floral context. Through their hybrid nature they add something new to the ornament families known up to now.

PAST
Widespread in all ornamentally advanced cultures, FLORAL: ARCHETYPES offers a formal response to needs that were once considered significant but today are largely unknown. Such shapes, which are presently regarded as enigmatic, were not created by designers, but instead come from a different, buried context. Engaging precisely because they were not designed, their forms continue to send a message today.

6   See translator's note on p. 332.

3.   Floral
3.3 Archetypes   3.3.1 with Sine Waves

For the first time since the Rococo period, the SINE
WAVE again evolves as an independent ornamental
form. By adding two, three, four or five sine waves,
twenty-five object-free forms emerge, some with
representational associations.

PRESENT
The SINE WAVE asserts itself as timeless in both a
short form and as an endless wave among ornamental shapes recognized as a World Cultural Heritage.
Vertically it serves as an icon for torrential rain and
horizontally as an icon for water and wave. It is found
in logos, coats of arms (e.g., that of the German state
of North Rhine–Westphalia) or on tiled roofs.

PAST
The SINE WAVE, decorated with LEAVES and
FLOWERS, is familiar to many cultures. In the early
nineteenth century, the French discovered ornamen-
tal Islamic art in Egypt, erroneously calling it "Art
Arab" and thus referring to the SINE WAVE as
"Arabesque." SINE WAVES enjoyed a heyday in
Rococo, when they became the main ornament in the
so-called rocaille style, with a shell-like spiral at one
end and a "feather" at the other.

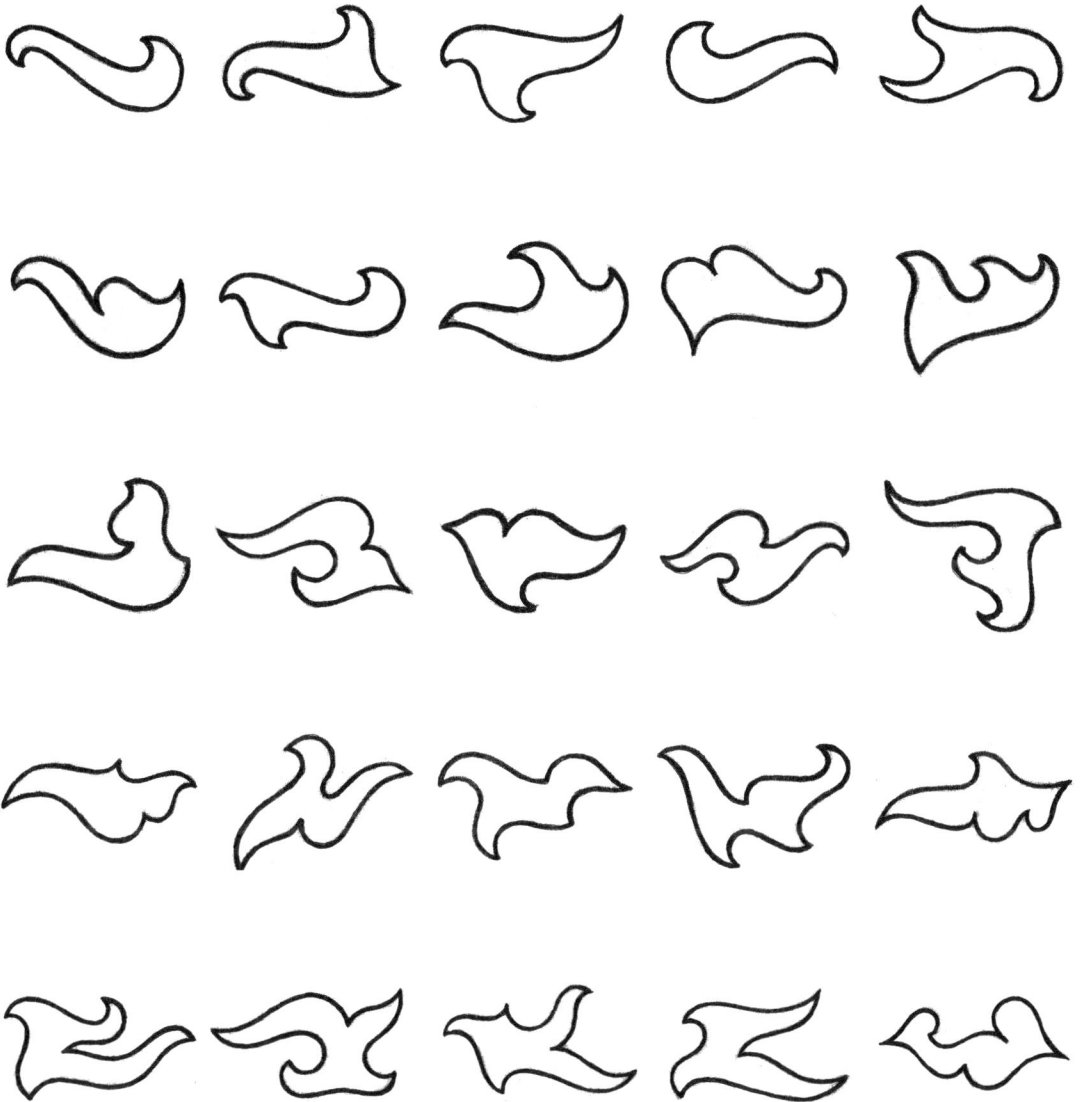

1

2

3

4

5

6

3. Floral
3.3 Archetypes

3.3.2 with Ovals

As an OVAL or (almond-shaped) mandorla (ovaloid), the energy-filled shape of FLORAL: ARCHETYPES with OVALS is best expressed in a free arrangement. The unconscious knowledge of the concentrated life energy it contains is also expressed in a spontaneous perception: an OVAL with a shape drawn in only two dimensions nevertheless creates a three-dimensional effect.

PRESENT
OVAL comes from the Latin ovum, egg. An egg depicts a single cell magnified many times. The life-giving properties inside the shell cannot be seen but can be perceived intuitively.

PAST
Known since the ancient Greeks as an element in architectural decorations, the OVAL enjoys its annual high point in the mountains of eggs on Easter in the Christian world.

3.3.2 with Ovals
Detail of an artwork by Achim
Zeman, *In motion 06*, acrylic paint,
cast resin and wood, 2018

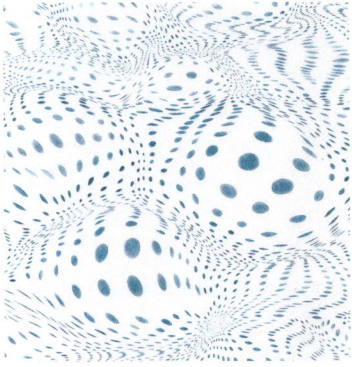

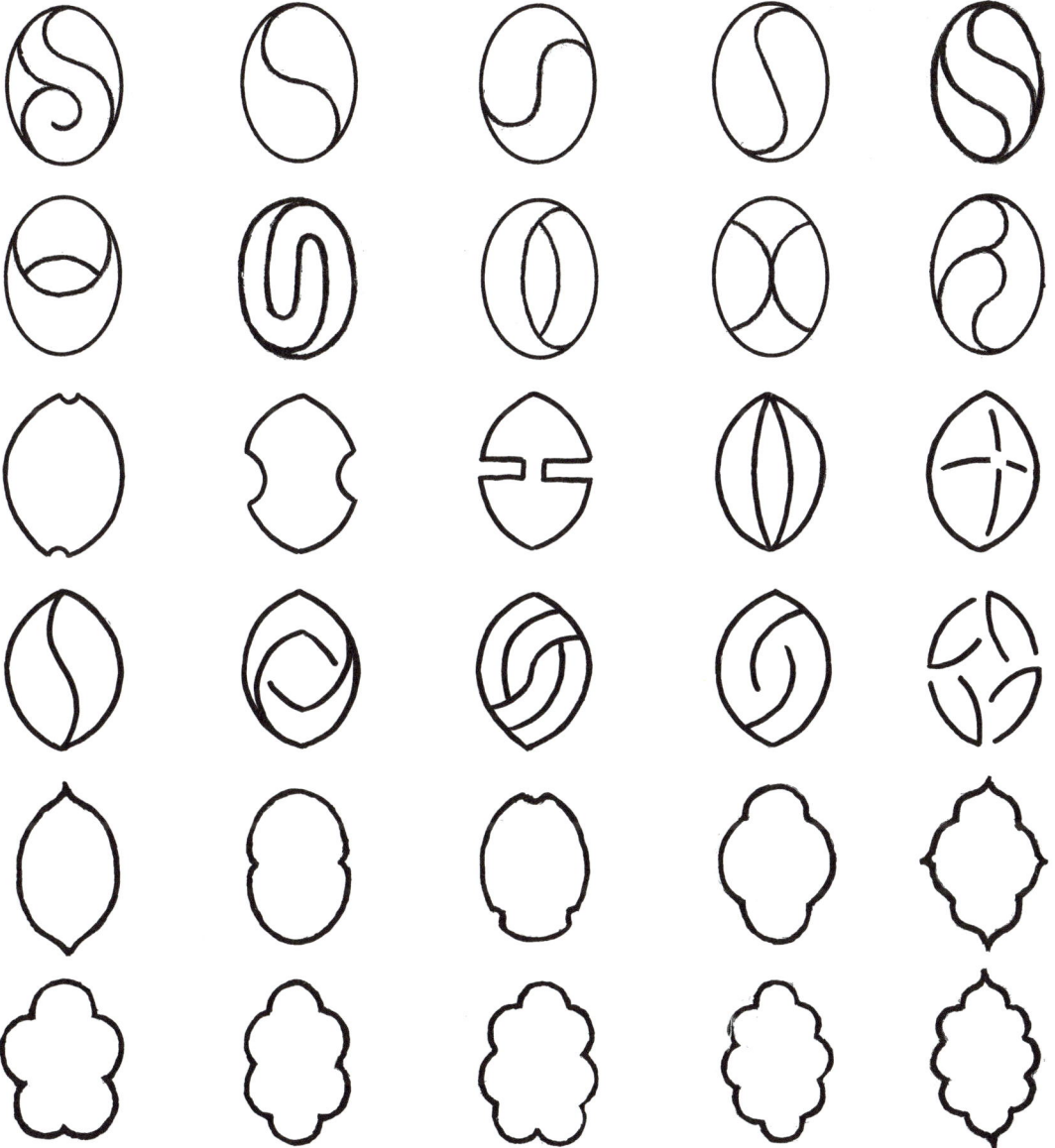

1

2

3

1 Combination with MISCELLANEOUS forms
2 Combination of all ovaloid forms

3 Combination of all OVAL forms
4 Combination of all OVAL forms

5 Combination of all mandorla (ovaloid) forms

3.   Floral
3.3   Archetypes

3.3.3 with Spirals

Two arrangements of SPIRAL shapes are shown: closed individual shapes and shapes that merge and are multiply twisted in each other.

PRESENT
The most famous SPIRAL, a snail's shell, has seven whorls, but ornaments depict a maximum of only two. The theme is often a reference to unfolding and waning life energy.

PAST
In antiquity, viewing a double SPIRAL (one clockwise and one counterclockwise) was seen as defensive magic. It was intended to interrupt the viewer's thoughts. This form can still be seen today on Greek fishing boats.

3.3.3   with Spirals
Cast-iron fence, Stoclet Palace,
Brussels, 20th century

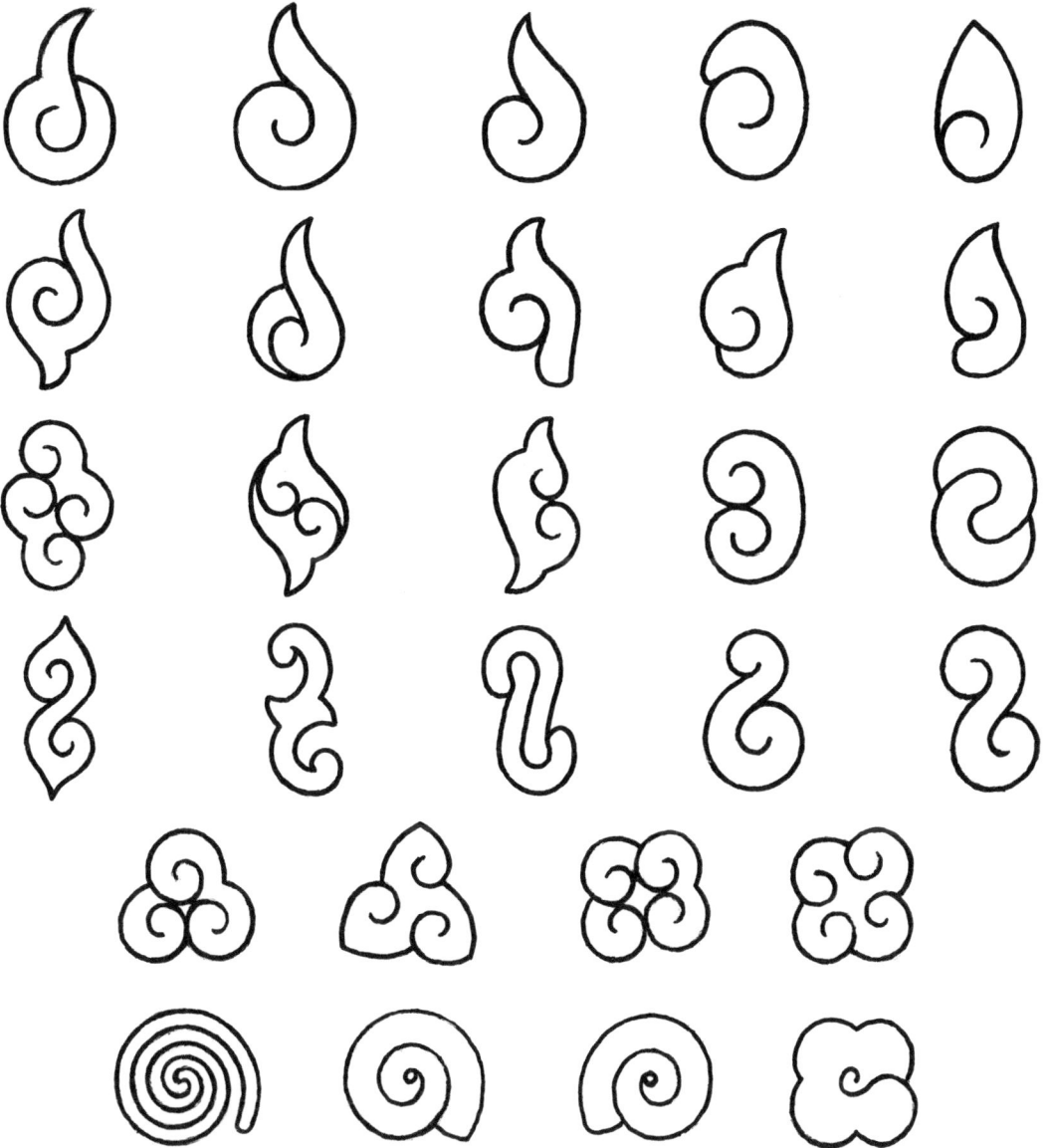

1

3

5   Color variation of Figure 2

3   Combination of variations
4   SPIRALS in DOTS and LINES

1   SPIRALS on a 60-degree grid
2   SPIRALS in DOTS and LINES

3. Floral
3.3 Archetypes

3.3.4 Miscellaneous

The mystery emanating from such individual shapes stimulates the imagination and can lead to new families of ornaments.

PRESENT
The twenty-four individual shapes gathered here do not comprise a family, with the exception of the boteh motif. Instead they are a loosely related group. Known up to now mostly in ethnological or esoteric contexts, FLORAL: ARCHETYPES MISCELLANEOUS is now given its own ornamental platform for the first time.

PAST
One often encounters these individual shapes in historical World Cultural Heritage ornamental shapes. This can be assumed to trace back to a lost collective context that can be rediscovered when examined more closely. Best known is boteh (Persian), an androgynous shape mainly woven into Kashmir shawls. In the nineteenth century, this pattern was replicated by a weaving factory in the town of Paisley, in Scotland.

3.3.4 Miscellaneous
Detail of a Turkish woven silk cloth,
15th century

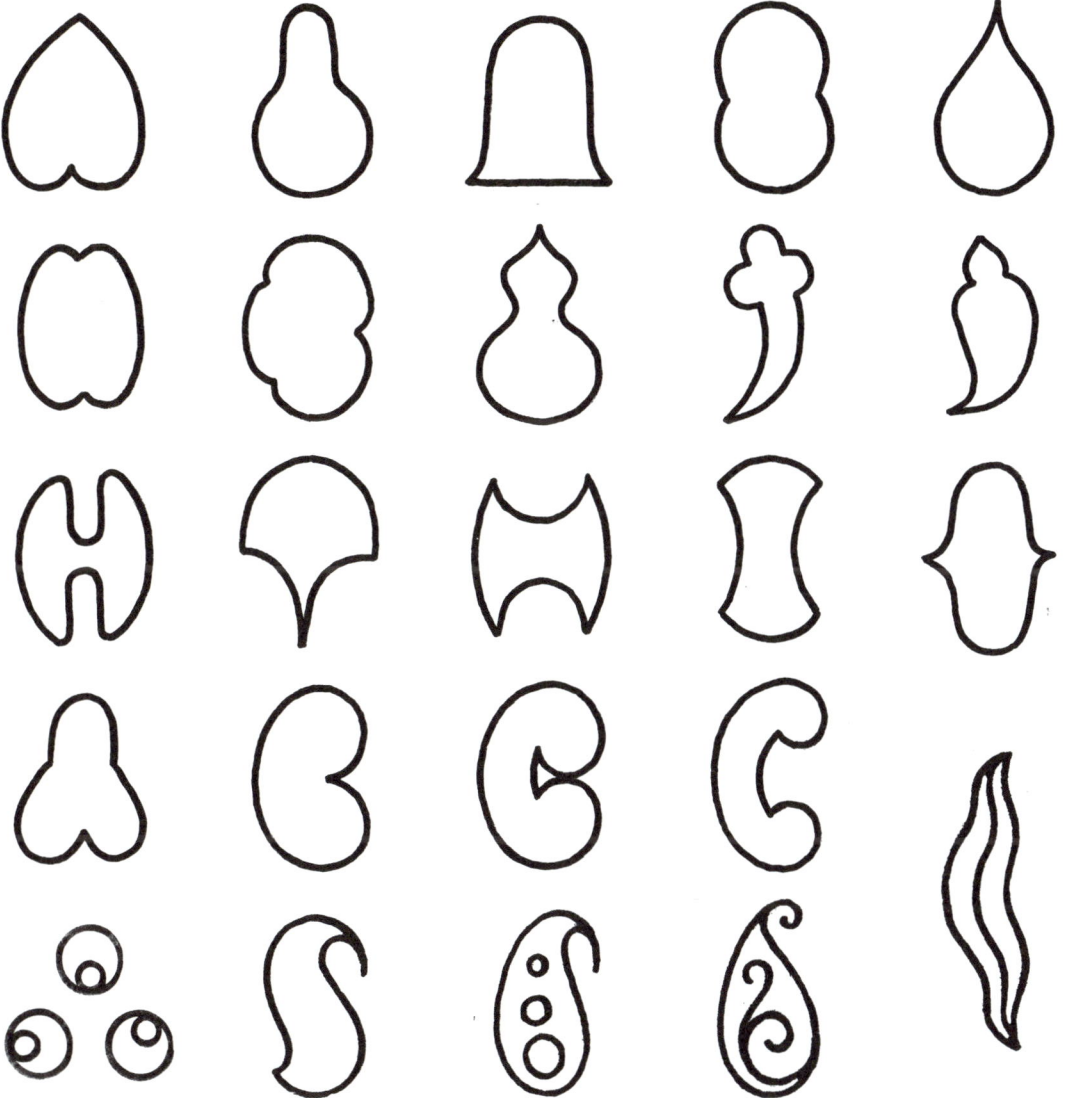

1

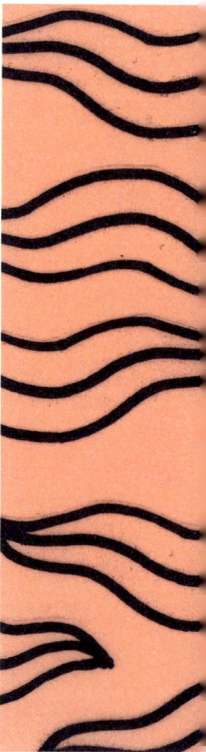

3

2

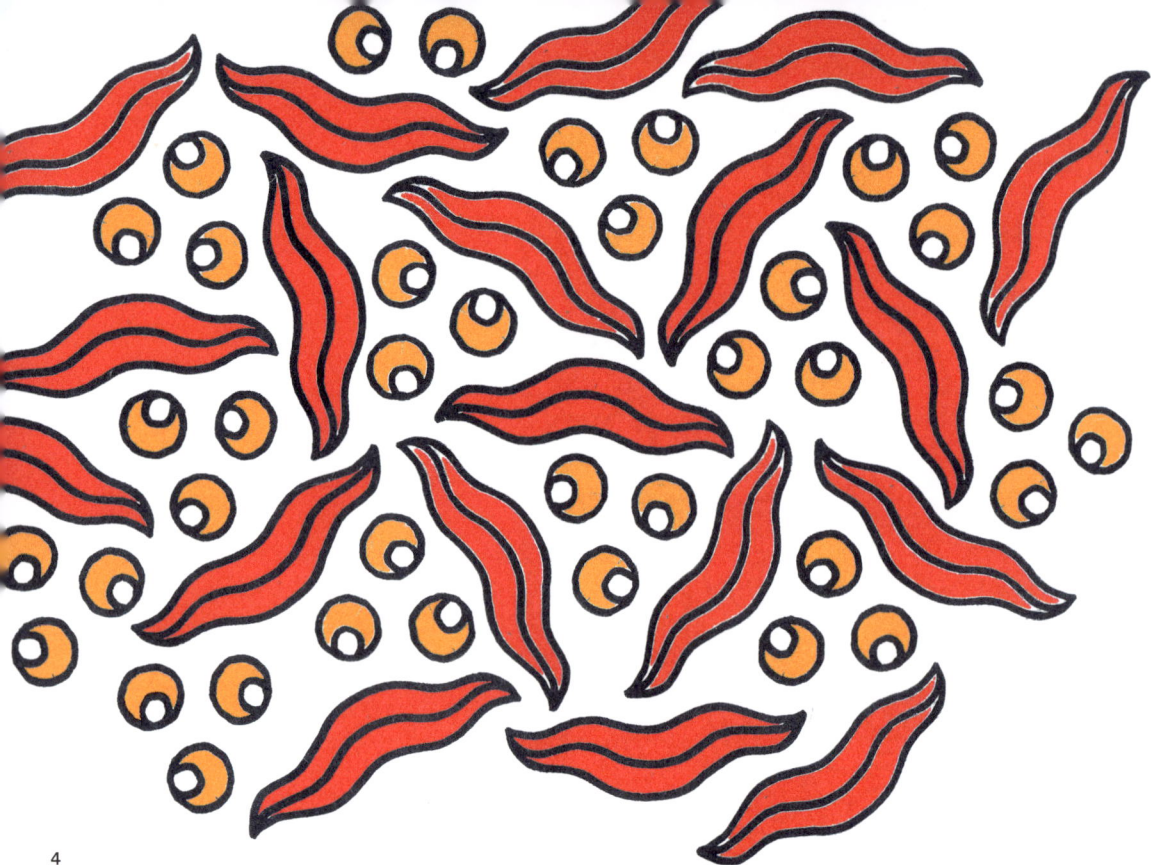

4

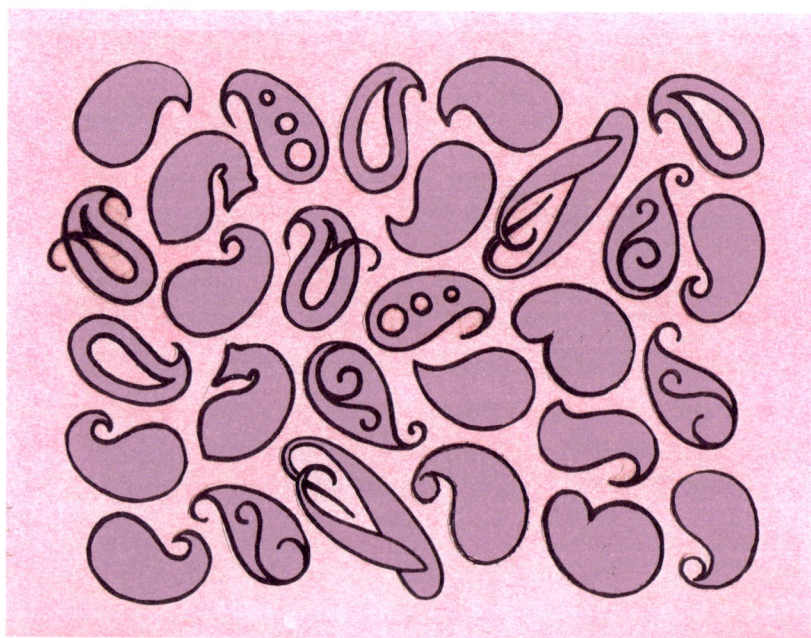

5

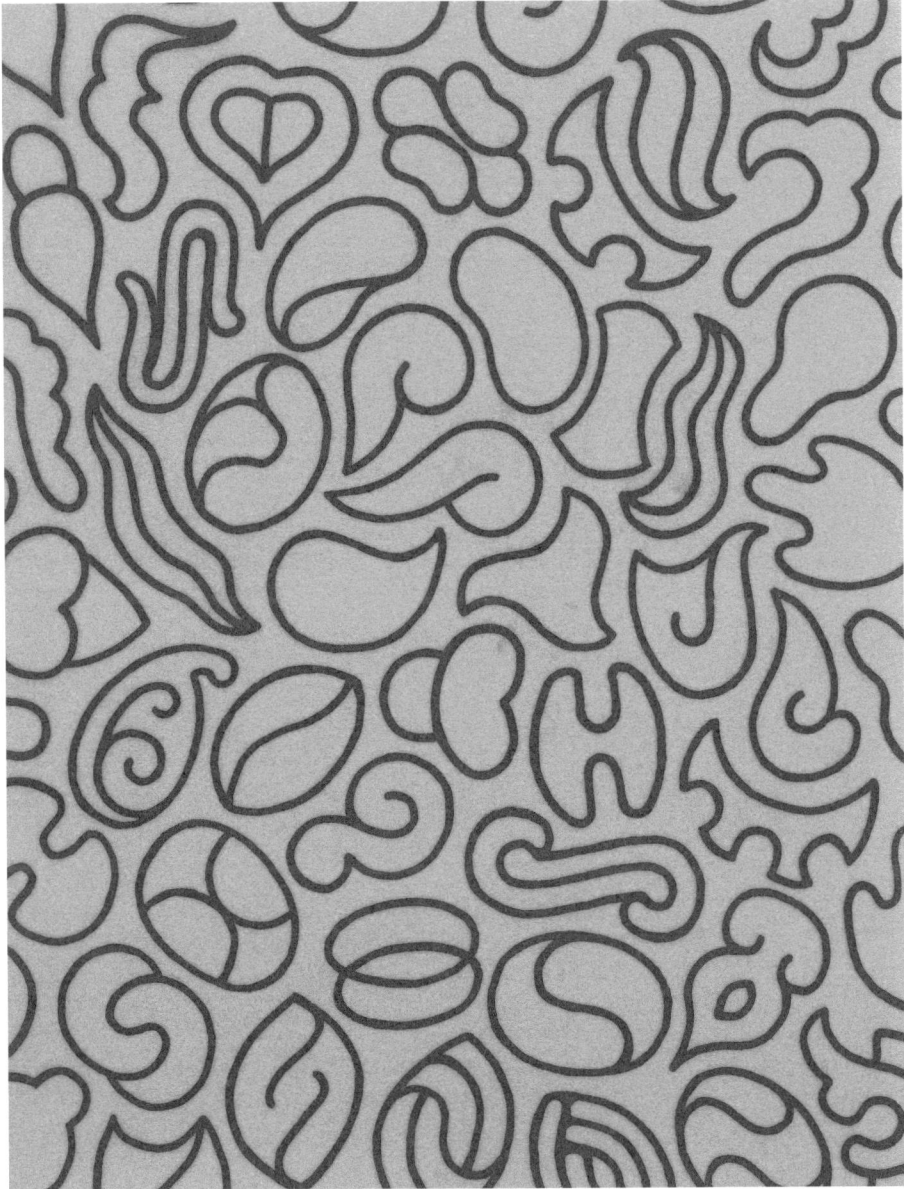

1 Combination with boteh variations
2 Combination of Japanese triangular clan symbols
3 Combination of one part of a Turkish cintamani pattern
4 Combination of Turkish cintamani on a triangular grid
5 Combination of boteh variations
6 Combination with OVALS (page 238)

6

For the first time, formations of clouds, water, fire and landscapes are broken down into individual, distinct shapes, making separate compilations possible.

PRESENT
Cloud formations, waterfalls, large waves with landscape panoramas fading into the distance and less frequently blazing fires are often depicted on screens and wall paintings, mostly in the Far East.

PAST
When Chinese and Japanese scroll paintings, screens, ceramics and gardens became known in Europe between the mid-eighteenth and the late nineteenth centuries, it triggered a new artistic style there, chinoiserie. During the period of Japanism, the Japanese artist Hokusai became well known for his colored woodblock prints of flowing water and fading landscapes. Persian book illumination also provided new ornamental artwork, with its images of cloud formations, inspired by the Mongolian sky, its landscapes and the representation of fire.

3.4 Earth
Based on a Persian illumination,
15th century

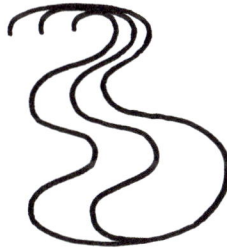

1

2

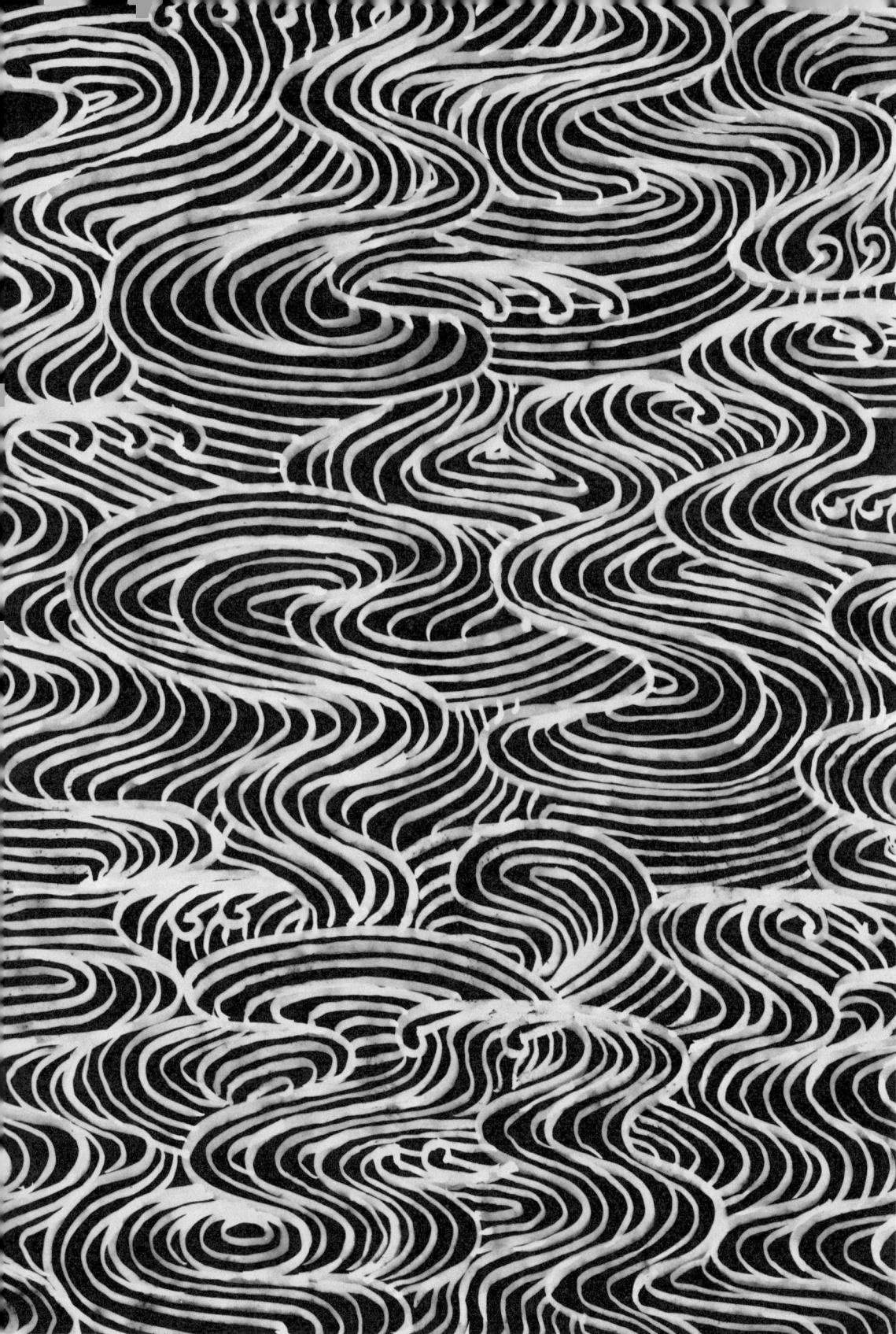

323   Floral: Archetype

Air, Water, Fire and Earth

5

6

8

10

1 Combination of the six CLOUD shapes with DOTS
2 Combination of the six CLOUD shapes, linear
3 Combination of the three WAVE shapes, closely spaced lines
4 Combination of the three WAVE shapes, widely spaced lines
5 Combination of the five FIRE shapes with volume
6 Combination of the five FIRE shapes, linear
7 Japanese mulberry tree veneer
8 Grass based on a Japanese model
9 Bamboo based on a Japanese model
10 Steppe grass, developed from a model by Sonia Delaunay

Air, Water, Fire and Earth

In *New Grammar of Ornament* I would like to offer a stimulus to reconsider ornamentation systematically based on its previous history. In doing that, I will be looking not only at the early history, but also at the ornament cultures that have evolved worldwide. Despite my view of the boundless wealth of this World Cultural Heritage of Ornament, my examination will have to remain selective, for my interest in ornament is marked by my background.

Even in my youth I could not comprehend the constant demonization of ornamentation by adult artists and art enthusiasts. This was vehement, though all the households of artists that I grew up in did have highly valued ornamental objects, whether African weavings, Persian fabrics, rugs, miniatures or Chinese ceramics.

Through a series of coincidences, my interest in Islamic-Persian ornaments started growing. First of all, at fifteen I discovered a book by the Orient scholars Heinrich Glück and Ernst Diez about the architecture of the Seljuks in the Turkish city of Konya. I was visually familiar with abstract and constructive art, but there for the first time I saw constructive art in connection with architecture. That proved to set a crucial impetus in motion, which later led me to study architecture at the Technical University of Munich.

After graduating and completing my study of the geometricizing architectural style of Louis Khan, I soon started working for Kamran Diba in Iran, for Hassan Fathy in Egypt and for Aga Khan in London.

Yet my architectural style based on Persian geometry was not enough for me. As of 1986 I wanted to work with the newly discovered ornamental geometry in Europe. My contacts to the architectural scene gave me the opportunity to work on major "Kunst-am-Bau" (Art in Architecture) projects. Together with Claudia Weil, I published my basic research on the geometric ornament in *Ornament in Architecture, Art and Design* in 2004.

Soon afterwards my interest in floral ornamentation was piqued. With the idea of a set of building blocks and the subject of archetypes, I started a new group of works with rug collections and oil paintings. When I was offered a teaching position at a Munich Design Academy in 2007, I developed a study program on ornament. I noticed how difficult it was to convey my elitist artistic ornamental style. Being accustomed to collecting and collaging important visual ideas in photographs, I started organizing them under the aspect of GEOMETRIC versus FLORAL and seeking simple arrangement principles. I discovered four prototypical groups: STRIPED, RECTANGULAR, TRIANGULAR and FREE order. As a third pillar of ornaments came MINIMAL, and the idea to develop a New Grammar.

I heard of the excavations near Cape Town, South Africa, in 2014. The artifacts corresponded to my identification of ornamental prototypes. They represent the earliest beginning for ornament and for art, both in a language free of any representation. Since 1500 CE in the European sphere, the fine arts had been appraised higher than ornament and after 1900 CE, ornament was abolished entirely. Artists rediscovered the anthropological constant, MINIMAL as an object-free art, and declared it to be modern art. For one hundred years already, it has been an established branch of the fine arts. In the late twentieth century, a renaissance of ornament surfaced in Europe. The other spheres – sub-Saharan Africa, Islam and the Far East – had not followed Europe in separating fine arts and ornament, and there the former practice has been maintained. For them all, I offer new directions of ornament and revive unfamiliar preexisting ones.

The constant back-and-forth between artist and ornament designer, between the two forms of aesthetics, thus suddenly had an important interface. My credo is: An ornament lacking criteria of art is just as pointless as an art that excludes the notion of order. With this book I provide this means, for ornament through art and for art through ornament. Popular and elitist, simple and complex, certain and uncertain, ornament and the liberal arts are two historically connected fields that have been wrongfully separated.

Biographies

Thomas Weil

· Artist, designer, architect, curator and author

· Born 1944 in Bavaria, Germany, sixth generation in an artist family

· Lives in Friedberg near Augsburg

· Starting 1964: studied architecture at the Technical University in Munich; worked as an architect until 1996 (incl. 1970–1972 Munich Olympic Village)

· Since 1970: concentration on geometric ornamentation in art, architecture, and design

· Starting 1976: traveled to Spain, Persia, Egypt, Saudi Arabia and Turkey

· 1979: started a friendship with architect Hassan Fathy from Cairo, until his death in 1989

· 1985: taught Islamic Ornamentics at Heluan Academy in Cairo

· Starting late 1970s: Designed and created interiors for C.H. Beck publishers in Munich (1978–1996) and for Aga Khan (Ismaili Center London, 1980–1984)

· Starting 1986: worked as an artist primarily in Kunst-am-Bau (Art in Architecture) projects (incl. Postbank Köln, Feuerwehr Krefeld); had paintings exhibited in museums and galleries (incl. W. Hack Museum, Ludwigshafen; Aedes Galerie, Berlin; Architekturgalerie, Munich); designed rugs (e.g., for Vorwerk, Anker Deutschland) and tile collections (Villeroy & Boch Germany).

· 2004: co-authored with Claudia Weil *Ornament in Architektur, Kunst und Design* (Munich: Callwey) and the American edition *Geometric Ornament in Architecture, Art and Design* (Altglen, PA: Schiffer, 2009)

· 2007–2017: teaching position on ornament at the Design Academy in Munich

· Starting 2005: in addition to lectures, teaching assignments, and publications, concentration on minimal, geometric and floral ornament

· 2017: on the initiative of designer Timo Weil, Boah Kim was commissioned to design the book *New Grammar Of Ornament*

· 2019: together with Timo Weil, made contact at the Frankfurt Book Fair with Lars Müller Publishers, Zurich, and the cooperative effort began in the spring of 2020.

Boah Kim

Boah Kim is a designer from Seoul, Korea. She is currently based in Paris, where she makes books and works as an art director. Craving Apollinaire's poems and concrete poetry introduced her to the world of typography. She believes in books as a matter of time-based media, where images and texts take part in creating stories organically. Apart from book creation, she works as a consultant and graphic designer for various fashion houses in Paris and worldwide. http://www.boah.kim/

Heinz Schütz

Heinz Schütz, Ph.D., is an art theorist, art critic, author and lecturer at various higher education institutions, including the University of Munich and the Munich Academy of Fine Arts. As an art critic, he wrote for *Süddeutsche Zeitung* and various trade journals; since 1987 he has been a staff correspondent for *Kunstforum international* and editor of the volumes *Transformation und Wiederkehr*, *Das Theater der Embleme*, *Kunst Geschichte Kunst*, *Urban Performance*, *Museumsboom* and *Act!*. He designed and curated the international research and exhibition project *Performing the City*. Dr. Schütz has published works on modern and contemporary art, was a guest lecturer at universities, and participated in symposia.

Manuel Will

Dr. Manuel Will is an archaeologist and paleoanthropologist at the University of Tübingen, with a research focus on the cultural and biological evolution of human beings in Africa. He presently leads archaeological excavations in Germany and South Africa, researching the material culture of *Homo sapiens* during the Paleolithic (Old Stone) Age. Dr. Will studied pre- and protohistorical archaeology and human evolution at the universities of Tübingen and Cambridge (UK), and completed a doctorate under Prof. Nicholas Conard in 2016 on the Stone Age in South Africa. From 2016 to 2018, he was a Research Fellow at the renowned Gonville & Caius College at Cambridge University in the Department of Archaeology and Anthropology. Since 2018, Dr. Will has been on the academic staff at the University of Tübingen in the Department of Early Prehistory and Quaternary Ecology.

Translator's Note

The author's aim to describe the different categories or principles of ornamentation as based on the proto-ornaments follows from his identification of these principles as anthropological constants, consisting of geometric forms but free of any representational figures. He called this quality *gegenstandsfrei*, literally "free of objects," which I had wanted to translate as "nonrepresentational" or "nonfigurative," as is common in art. But the author felt that a direct negation of representational or figurative art generally implies that there is an object in the background that is then rejected or abstracted from. In searching for an appropriate term, I came across Wassily Kandinsky's description of music and his seeing the task facing artists is to approach the state of music, which he referred to as "non-material," "need[ing] no outer form," "representing no object of reality":

"A painter who finds no satisfaction in the mere representation of natural phenomena, however artistic, ... enviously observes the simplicity and ease with which such an aim is already achieved in the non-material art of music. ... Music, by its very nature, is ultimately and fully emancipated and needs no outer form for its expression."
[*On the Spiritual in Art* (Guggenheim Foundation, 1946), 35-36]

"The other form remains abstract, that is, it represents no object of reality but in itself is a fully abstract being. Such purely abstract beings, which possess their own life, their own influence, and their own value, are a square, a circle, a triangle, a rhombus, a trapezoid, and innumerable other forms becoming more complicated with no mathematical designation. All these forms occupy space in the realm of the non-objective" [48].

"The observer must learn to look at the picture as a graphic representation of a *mood* and not as a representation of *objects*" [emphasis from Kandinsky, in K. C. Lindsay and P. Vergo, eds., *Kandinsky: Complete Writings on Art* (Boston: G. K. Hall, 1982), pp. 402 ff.]

Many authors have commented on this aspect in Kandinsky's art:

"Kandinsky repeatedly evokes music as an ideal for a more abstract, 'object-free' art."

"Kandinsky viewed music as the most transcendent form of non-objective art – musicians could evoke images in listeners' minds merely with sounds. He strove to produce similarly object-free, spiritually rich paintings."

Kasimir Malevich, too, expressed an "attempt to free art from the burden of the object," his art being described similarly, stressing the "geometric, 'object-free'" nature of his paintings, asserting that "Malevich did it with art without an object – object-free art."

We felt these descriptions corresponded well to the author's intention, so ornament that is free of any representation is referred to in the following as "object-free."

Allison Brown

332

Bibliography

General

Brüderlin, Markus et al.: *Kunst & Textil. Stoff als Material und Idee in der Moderne von Klimt bis heute / Art and Textiles: Fabric as Material and Concept in Modern Art from Klimt to the Present*, exhibition catalog, Kunstmuseum Wolfsburg and Staatsgalerie Stuttgart, Ostfildern: Hatje Cantz, 2013.

Ciuha, Celia: *Blumenmythos. Von Vincent van Gogh bis Jeff Koons / Flower Myth: Vincent van Gogh to Jeff Koons*, exhibition catalog, Fondation Beyeler, Riehen, Wolfratshausen: Edition Minerva, 2005.

Frutiger, Adrian: *Der Mensch und seine Zeichen*, Frankfurt am Main: D. Stempel AG, 1978.

Gombrich, Ernst: *Ornament und Kunst. Schmucktrieb und Ordnungssinn in der Psychologie des dekorativen Schaffens*, Stuttgart: Klett Cotta, 1982.

Graf, Otto Antonia: *Otto Wagner. Die Einheit der Kunst*, vol. 3, Vienna, Cologne and Weimar: Böhlau, 1990.

Jones, Owen: *The Grammar of Ornament*, reprint, New York: Van Nostrand Reinhold Co., 1972.

Larson, Jack Lenor et al.: *The Dyer's Art: Ikat, Batik, Plangi*, New York: Van Nostrand Reinhold Co., 1976.

Luhmann, Niklas: *Art as a Social System*, trans. Eva M. Knodt, Stanford, CA: Stanford University Press, 2000.

Prehistory

Critchlow, Keith: *Time Stands Still: New Light on Megalithic Science*, London: Fraser, 1979.

Gimbutas, Marija: *The Language of the Goddess: Unearthing the Hidden Symbols of Western Civilization*, San Francisco: Harper & Row, 1989.

König, Marie: *Am Anfang der Kultur. Die Zeichensprache des frühen Menschen*, Berlin: Gebrüder Mann, 1973.

Lenerz-De Wilde, Majolie: *Zirkelornament in der Kunst der Latènezeit*, Munich: C.H. Beck, 1977.

Sub-Saharan Africa

Courtney-Clark, Margaret: *Ndebele: The Art of an African Tribe*, New York: Rizzoli, 1986.

Fisher, Angela: *Africa Adorned*, London: William Collins, 1984.

Fondation Dapper: *Au Royaume du Signe. Appliqués sur toile des Kuba, Zaïre*, exhibition catalog, Musée Dapper, Paris, Paris: Editions Adam Biro and Editions Dapper, 1988.

Meurant, Georges: *Shoowa Design: African Textiles from the Kingdom of Kuba*, London: Thames & Hudson, 1986.

Meurant, Georges: *Traumzeichen. Raphiagewebe des Königreichs Bakuba*, Munich: Fred Jahn, 1989.

Sieber, Roy: *African Textiles and Decorative Arts*, exhibition catalog, The Museum of Modern Art, New York, 1972.

Europe

Balmelle, Catherine, and Richard Prudhomme: *Le décor géometrique de la mosaique romaine*, multilingual publication, Paris: Picard, 1985.

Clark, Fiona: *William Morris: Wallpapers and Chintzes*, London: Academy Editions, 1973.

Glass, Dorothy F.: *Studies on Cosmatesque Pavements*, British Archaeological Reports, Oxford, 1980.

Kapitza: *Geometric: Graphic Art and Pattern Fonts*, Mainz: Hermann Schmidt, 2008.

Kier, Hiltrud: *Der mittelalterliche Schmuckfussboden*, Düsseldorf: Rheinland-Verlag, 1970.

Meller, Susan, and Joost Elffers: *Textile Designs: 200 Years of Patterns for Printed Fabrics*, London: Thames & Hudson, 2010.

Schmidt, Petra, Annette Tietenberg, and Ralf Wollheim, eds.: *Patterns. Muster in Design, Kunst und Architektur / Patterns in Design, Art and Architecture*, Basel: Birkhäuser, 2007.

Far East

Blakemore, Frances: *Japanese Design through Textile Patterns*, New York: Weatherhill, 1989.

Brandt, Klaus (ed.): *Nô. Gewänder und Masken des japanischen Theaters*, exhibition catalog, Museum Rietberg, Zürich, Linden-Museum, Stuttgart, and Kultur- und Stadthistorisches Museum, Duisburg, Stuttgart, 1993.

Dye, Daniel Sheets: *Chinese Lattice Designs*, reprint, New York: Dover Publications, 1974.

Kahlenberg, Mary Hunt et al.: *Asian Costumes and Textiles from the Bosphorus to Fujiyama: The Zaira and Marcel Mis Collection*, Milan: Skira, 2001.

Kennedy, Alan: *Japanese Costume: History and Tradition*, Paris: Adam Biro, 1990.

Noma, Seiroku: *Japanese Costume and Textile Arts*, New York/ Tokyo: Weatherhill/Heibonsha, 1974.

Ouchi, Hajime: *Japanese Optical and Geometrical Art*, New York: Dover Publications, 1977.

Roojen, Pepin van: *Indonesian ornamental Design*, Amsterdam: Pepin Press, 1998.

Wang, Fushi et al.: *Ethnic Costumes and Clothes Decorations from China*, Hong Kong: Hai Feng Publishing, 1986.

Islam

Atasoy, Nurhan et al.: *Ipek, The Crescent and the Rose: Imperial Ottoman Silks and Velvets*. London: Azimuth Editions, 2001.

Bourgoin, Jules: *Arabic Geometrical Pattern and Design*, reprint, New York: Dover Publications, 1973.

Clévenot Dominique, and Gérard Degeorge: *Splendors of Islam: Architecture, Decoration, and Design*, trans. Jean Davis, New York: Vendome Press, 2000 [French original: *Décors d'Islam*, Paris: Editions Citadelles et Mazenod, 2000].

El-Said, Issam and Ayse Parman: *Geometric Concepts in Islamic Art*, London: World of Islam Festival Publishing Co., 1976.

Michaud, Roland, Sabrina Michaud, and Michael Barry: *Colour and Symbolism in Islamic Architecture*, London: Thames & Hudson, 1996 [French original: *Faïences d'azur*, Paris: Imprimerie Nationale, 1995].

Öney, Gönül, and Banri Namikawa: *Turkish Ceramic Tile Art*, Tokyo: Heibousha, 1975.

Paccard, André: *Traditional Islamic Craft in Moroccan Architecture*, trans. Mary Guggenheim [French original: *Le Maroc et l'artisanat traditionnel islamique dans l'architecture*], Saint-Jorioz: Editions Atelier 74, 1980.

Pope, Arthur: *Persian Architecture*, London: Thames & Hudson, 1965.

Schneider, Gerd: *Geometrische Bauornamente der Seldschuken in Kleinasien*, Wiesbaden: Reichert, 1980.

Schneider, Gerd: *Pflanzliche Bauornamente der Seldschuken in Kleinasien*, Wiesbaden: Reichert, 1989.

Seher-Thoss, Sonja and Hans Seherr-Thoss: *Design and Color in Islamic Architecture*, Washington, D.C.: Smithsonian Institution, 1968.

Wade, David: *Pattern in Islamic Art*, London: Studio Vita, 1976.

Walker, Daniel: *Flowers Underfoot: Indian Carpets of the Mughal Era*, exhibition catalog, Metropolitan Museum of Art, New York, London: Thames & Hudson, 1997.

Thomas Weil
NEW GRAMMAR OF ORNAMENT

www.ornamentconcepts.de

Concept & Design
Boah Kim | www.boah.kim
Translations and copyediting (English)
Allison Brown
Copyediting (German)
Sandra Leitte
Proofreading
Kristie Kachler
Editorial coordination
Maya Rüegg
Claudia Weil

Lithography
prints professional, Berlin, Germany
Printing and binding
DZA Druckerei zu Altenburg, Germany
Paper
LonaOffset 120 gsm

Lars Müller Publishers is supported by the Swiss Federal Office of Culture with a structural contribution for the years 2021–2024.

Lars Müller Publishers
Zurich, Switzerland
www.lars-mueller-publishers.com

Distributed in North America by ARTBOOK | D.A.P.
www.artbook.com

Printed in Germany
ISBN 978-3-03778-653-6

The publisher has endeavored to identify all copyright holders and photographers. Should despite our intensive research any person entitled to rights have been overlooked, they are kindly requested to contact the publisher.

Sponsors

Gabriele und Peter Breidenbach

CLAYTEC®
Baustoffe aus Lehm

ArnoBuchegger
Stiftung

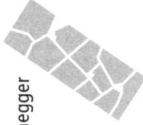

Image Credits

All images are © Thomas Weil, except as indicated below.

p. 6 (right)   Reprinted from *Journal of Archaeological Science* 35 (6), Mackay, A., & A. Welz, "Engraved ochre from a middle stone age context at Klein Kliphuis in the Western Cape of South Africa," pp.1521–1532, Copyright (2008), with permission from Elsevier.
p. 7 (left)   Reprinted from *Proceedings of the National Academy of Sciences* 107 (14), Texier, P. J., G. Porraz, J. Parkington, J. P. Rigaud, C. Poggenpoel, C. Miller, and C. Verna (2010), pp. 6180–6185, with permission from PNAS.
p. 7 (right)   Reprinted from *Quaternary international* 491, Dutkiewicz, E., S. Wolf, & N. J. Conard, "Early symbolism in the Ach and the Lone valleys of southwestern Germany," pp. 30–45, Copyright (2018), with permission from Elsevier.
p. 8   © Universität Tübingen / Photo: Hilde Jensen
p. 9   Reprinted from *Journal of Archaeological Science: Reports* 13, Guéret, C., & A. Bénard, "'Fontainebleau rock art' (Ile-de-France, France), an exceptional rock art group dated to the Mesolithic? Critical return on the lithic material discovered in three decorated rock shelters," pp. 99–120, Copyright (2017), with permission from Elsevier.
p. 10 (left)   © Association Marcel Duchamp / 2021, ProLitteris, Zurich. Photo: © bpk / Staatsgalerie Stuttgart
p. 10 (right)   Photo: Heinz Schütz
p. 11   Photo: Locutus Borg / CC BY-SA3.0
pp. 12–13   public domain
pp. 14–15   © 2021, ProLitteris, Zurich
p. 41 (middle)   Photo: Tony Hisgett / CC BY 2.0
p. 113 (right)   Photo: Satoru Mishima
p. 285   © Roland et Sabrina MICHAUD/GAMMA RAPHO
p. 259   © The Andy Warhol Foundation for the Visual Arts, Inc. / 2021, ProLitteris, Zurich
p. 265   © Judy Ledgerwood, 2021 / courtesy of the artist and Rhona Hoffman Gallery
p. 301   Courtesy of Achim Zeman